101 Activities for

Siblings Who

Squabble

DISCARDED

101 Activities for Siblings Who Squabble

Projects and Games to Entertain and Keep the Peace

Linda Williams Aber

Illustrations by Elaine Yabroudy

St. Martin's Griffin / New York
A Skylight Press Book

1668997

j
GV
1203
A22
1995

101 ACTIVITIES FOR SIBLINGS WHO SQUABBLE: PROJECTS AND GAMES TO
ENTERTAIN AND KEEP THE PEACE. Copyright © 1995 by Skylight Press.
All rights reserved. Printed in the United States of America. No part
of this book may be used or reproduced in any manner whatsoever
without written permission except in the case of brief quotations
embodied in critical articles or reviews. For information, address
St. Martin's Press, 175 Fifth Avenue, New York, N.Y. 10010.

Published by arrangement with Skylight Press, 260 West 72nd
Street, Suite 6C, New York, N.Y. 10023.

Library of Congress Cataloging-in-Publication Data

Aber, Linda Williams.
    101 activities for siblings who squabble / Linda Williams Aber.
      p. cm.
    ISBN 0-312-13101-1
    1. Amusements.   2. Creative activities and seat work.
    3. Brothers and sisters.   I. Title.
    GV1203.A22   1995
    790.1—dc20   95-7937
                                               CIP

First St. Martin's Griffin Edition: June 1995

10 9 8 7 6 5 4 3 2 1

For Corey Mackenzie Aber and
Kip Alexander Aber

◆

◆ Contents ◆

Fre-e-e-e-e-zing Fun!

◆ Chapter 7: Sick of Being Sick
Boredom Blasters

Get Busy, Get Better

Pencil Sharpeners

◆ Chapter 8: The Gang's All Here
Fun for Sets of Siblings

All for Fun

◆ Chapter 9: Fence Menders
Games to Play and Things to Say for the "Not Speaking"

Fence Menders

101 Activities for Siblings Who Squabble

◆ Chapter 1 ◆

Ready, Set, Go!

Who's on First? What's on Second? And Where Do We Go from Here?

IN THE HISTORY OF the world and all its siblings, a fight-free existence is as rare as a hen that lays golden eggs. Until now. *101 Activities for Siblings Who Squabble* introduces games, activities, and argument enders that turn sibling rivalry into sibling revelry.

Children separated in age by one or more years can present a playtime challenge to parents who aren't prepared to address the differences in interests created by differences in ages. Some parents just accept it as a fact that kids of different ages don't play well together, fight a lot, and can't really do much more together than watch television. But this book is filled with alternatives to passive play. Each chapter offers suggestions for making the activities and games work well for a variety of ages.

Siblings can play happily together if they are taught how to make adjustments to one another's differing ability levels. Older siblings should be told in advance that the younger brother or sister may not be able to do something one way, but he or she can do it another way and the game can still work. Older brothers and sisters will naturally be better at certain things, but younger siblings can be bolstered in advance by hearing that trying their best is more important than winning. Everyone participating should understand that game plans can be changed to make play fairer.

Siblings will be siblings, and that only means that brothers and sisters, sisters and sisters, brothers and brothers, all have the same instincts: to survive, to be favored, to be *right!* In play as well as in work, children, siblings, friends, want to succeed, to win, and to be respected. Differences in ages can mean a difference in physical strength, muscle coordination, and energy level. They can also mean a difference in the ability to concentrate, follow directions, and communicate. Learning to be patient and understanding of one another's abilities and limitations is as important as learning the rules of any game.

This book is divided into nine chapters of cooperative games and activities chosen with the idea of bringing different ages into the same plane of happy coexistence. You'll find quiet games and activities, active play ideas for rainy day fun, and things to do on hot days, cold days, sick days, company days, and even during those terrible times when the siblings are so mad they can't even speak to each other.

To make peace more possible, "Argument Enders" are offered where appropriate. Each game and activity in this collection is accompanied by sections called "Different Ages, Different Stages" and "Then Try This!" These offer suggestions for ways to bend the rules for the benefit of younger siblings and to add variety for everyone. There are useful ideas for providing extra challenges to easier games so that older siblings won't cry "Too babyish!" when asked to play with a younger child. Appropriate ages are given under each activity title. These are suggestions only. Individual parents must determine their own children's level of ability and responsibility.

When there's nothing to do, there's plenty to do—indoors, outdoors, in tight spaces, and all places. When individual needs are considered and accommodated, new games are learned, but more important, mutual respect is gained. Let the games and activities begin fairly, squarely, and happily, of course.

SOCIAL SKILLS BUILDERS

Before quality playtime can begin, social skills need to be preached and practiced. Parents can do a lot to help siblings recognize one another as friends and playmates. By setting an example of being socially skilled persons, parents can teach their children some very valuable lessons.

Some siblings may feel "stuck" playing with one another. Resentment, competition for attention, and simple immaturity can make siblings mistreat each other. But to be happy in social situations, children need to know how to compromise, how to show respect for others, how to forgive and apologize, and how to control their own urges to be too aggressive. Here are some important things to understand and practice for happier social relationships.

- Listen to your children when they are talking to you. Don't interrupt or finish their sentences for them. This will teach them how to be good listeners too.
- Reinforce good behavior by pointing it out and complimenting your children on the way they behaved positively toward other children.
- If your children are too aggressive or are rude to one another or another person, speak to them about it in private. Try to make your children understand how such behavior makes another person feel.
- Teach your children some simple diplomatic ways to handle play situations. Children who learn that placing blame serves no purpose in playtime will spend less time fighting and more time playing. Diplomacy is a social skill that will come in handy all their lives.

If children can't agree on what game to play, suggest that one or the other say, "Try it for five minutes. If you don't like it we'll play something else."

If taking turns is a problem, suggest that the one being slighted say, "The game is more fun for all of us if we take turns. It's my turn now."

If one child teases or belittles another, suggest that the one being teased put a stop to it immediately by saying, "Let's try not to hurt each other's feelings. It spoils the fun in the game."

If diplomatic phrases don't stop crankiness or bad moods, a calm suggestion of a five-minute time-out in separate spaces often allows the players to start over happily.

WINNING WORDS

A good sport is the most important thing a player can be. Other players will always want to play again if the one who wins makes the ones who lose feel good about themselves. It's nice to be nice. Everybody benefits from hearing kind words. Here are some things children can be taught to say to playmates who have lost the game but not the respect and friendship of the winner.

- "Good game. You were tough competition."
- "Thanks for playing. It's your turn to win the next game!"
- "It was a close game. Better luck next time!"
- "I had a lot of fun. I hope you had fun too."

LOSING WORDS

Losing is never the best part about playing a game. Sometimes a player may be at a loss for words after losing. Before the tears well up, children can express their feelings with words that show that even though they are not thrilled about losing, they are not sore losers.

- "Congratulations. I wish I had won, but you really played a great game."

- "Let's play again and see who wins this time."
- "Good job. How about teaching me some of your tricks?"

FAIR STARTS

Choosing who's first in a game can be as much fun as the game itself. Here are some time-tested ways for determining playing order fairly and squarely.

- For two players, flip a coin. Players call out heads or tails. Heads goes first. Tails goes second.
- For two or more players, draw straws cut into different lengths. The longest straw goes first, and the order continues from longest to shortest, with the shortest being last.
- For large groups, saying some version of the "Eeny, meeny, miney, mo" verse helps to determine who is in and who is out. The one choosing says the rhyme and points to a different player on each word. The pointing goes back and forth among players, with the finger landing on someone at the end of the rhyme, counting that player out. The player left is "It." Here is the verse as it is best known:

> Eeny, meeny, miney, mo
> Catch a tiger by the toe
> If he hollers let him go
> Eeny, meeny, miney, mo.
> My mother says to pick this one,
> and you are not "It."

- In card games, the player drawing the highest card from the deck goes first, or the player sitting to the left of the dealer may go first.

STOP FIGHTING AND START PLAYING

All players of all ages would rather play than fight and argue. Clever comebacks often cut through the tension, but no words end an argument better than simply saying "I'm sorry." And no words keep the peace better than "Please," "Thank you," and

"You're welcome." When arguments begin, the best argument ender is an apology and a smile. Showing respect, care, and consideration for fellow players is the real key to having fun.

ARGUMENT ENDERS

Before playing begins there are definite rules for social behavior that need to be taught. Parents should make it clear to players that there are some things that are just not allowed: no name-calling, no sarcasm, no comparing, no negative comments.

Ending arguments is a social skill that can easily be learned. When a parent is called in to be the mediator, there are some specific concepts to remember and use for effective problem solving. When breaking up a dispute, speak in short, precise sentences. Don't look for blame, but listen closely to what the problem might really be (that is, one sibling is bullying the other, one sibling feels inferior to the other, one sibling is jealous of the other's ability, one sibling feels persecuted, and so forth). As the mediator, a parent must be respectful and courteous to both parties. Stick to the topic at hand, use positive language that acknowledges your understanding of the situation ("I see you are both upset. You're both good at things, but perhaps you feel she is doing this thing better than you are today"), and use the specific "Argument Enders" offered throughout this book for some of the more common arguments engaged in by siblings and friends.

SURPRISE SUPPLIES BOX

Just as diplomacy, respect, kindness, and consideration are important tools to bring to any games or activities, there are some basic craft and game supplies that any well-stocked home with children should have. Here are suggestions for things to put into the Surprise Supplies Box.

For Crafts Projects:
- plain paper
- construction paper
- pencils
- crayons
- markers
- paper clips
- tape
- glue
- yarn, string
- cardboard boxes
- fabric swatches
- paper bags
- old magazines
- paper cups
- paper plates
- food coloring
- scissors

For Games:
- playing cards
- paper
- pencils
- timer or stopwatch
- tape measure
- dice
- playground ball
- small rubber ball
- chalk

Keep the Surprise Supplies Box within easy reach so players can help themselves to the supplies they need. Every once in a while, refill and update the supplies so the box doesn't become just another "junk box."

♦ **Chapter 2** ♦

Shhhh! Don't Wake Anyone!

Quiet Fun for All Ages

"QUIET!" "SHHHH!" "HUSH!" All the whisper-please words in the world won't keep the noise down if the children are up! Whether the reason for turning your home into a "quiet zone" is a mom or dad working at home, a sibling home sick and sleeping upstairs, a baby asleep in a crib, or an elderly visitor requiring quiet in the house, those who are not working, not sleeping, and not looking to fill time with silence need to have their fun. The games and activities in this chapter are selected with two things in mind: peaceful sleeping for the sleepers, and peaceful playing for the players. Even when "mum" is the word, "fun" can be the other word!

GOING TO THE GAMES

You don't need fancy board games for kids who are just plain bored. All you need are some time-tested games that are easy

8

to explain and even easier to play. These activities challenge the minds of even the youngest players. Next time boredom strikes, strike back by going right for the games!

◆ Don't Look, Touch! ◆

(AGES 4 AND UP)

1 or more players

Materials:
paper bag
fabric swatches, 2 of each texture (corduroy, felt, velvet, wool, burlap, cotton, nylon, etc.)
timer or stopwatch
crayons or markers

Object of the Game:
To reach into the bag and use fingers and hands only to find as many fabric swatch matches as possible.

How to Play:
The sense of touch provides hands-on fun in this fabric-match game. Letting fingers, not eyes, do the matching gives hands of all sizes something to do when space is limited. Preparation is easy. Let the players do it all!

Prepare for the game by collecting as many different textures of fabric as are available around the house. Cut the fabric into pieces no smaller than 3" × 3", making two of each fabric texture. Place the fabric swatches into a paper bag. Players take turns reaching into the bag without looking and try to pull out two matching fabric swatches. Allow from 30 to 45 seconds for each turn. As long as the player makes a match, his or her turn continues. The player with the most matches wins.

For extended playtime, add more fabric swatches of different textures, or increase the amounts to be matched to three of each fabric.

Different Ages, Different Stages:
Players of all ages will enjoy collecting the fabrics to be used in the game. Older siblings who are handy with scissors should do the cutting, while younger players can keep busy decorating the paper bag with crayons or markers.

Children ages 4 and older will be capable of succeeding at this match-up game. Younger children may take a little longer to feel around in the bag with their fingers. As a guideline, allow 45 seconds for players ages 4 to 6, and 30 seconds for players 7 and up.

Then Try This!
Turn this game into a size-recognition and money-learning experience. Change the texture of the game completely by replacing fabric swatches with coins. Put two of each size coin into a paper bag. The object of the game is to feel the coins and find their matches.

◆ Memory Fun ◆
(AGES 4 TO 10)

1 or more players

Materials:
large tray
10 to 20 small objects (toothbrush, marble, penny, miniature car, ring, etc.)
towel or cloth large enough to cover the tray
pencil and paper for each player

Object of the Game:
To study the tray of objects and remember as many of them as possible.

How to Play:
Setting up the game can be just as much fun as playing it. Siblings of all ages can help each other collect items to be used

in the game. A parent or other nonplaying person should choose objects from the collection and spread them out on the tray. Cover the tray with the towel so neither player gets a sneak peek. Place the tray between the players, where both can easily see everything. Remove the towel and allow players to memorize the objects on the tray for about 1 minute. When the memorizing minute is up, the tray should be covered again. Players may then write down what they remember. Players should be given a time limit of 3 minutes to remember and list objects. The player with the most complete list wins.

For extended playtime, keep changing the objects and start over.

Different Ages, Different Stages:
If there is a wide gap in the ages of the players, you may want to prepare two trays. Older children may be more capable of remembering more objects. For the player who is between the ages of 4 and 6, prepare a tray of 10 objects. For the player between the ages of 7 and 10, prepare a tray of 20 objects. Assign a 2-point value to each item on the 10-object tray, and 1 point value to each item on the 20-object tray. Winners may be determined by highest point score.

If a younger player cannot write down answers alone, either the parent or the older sibling may help out by allowing the younger player to dictate answers.

Then Try This!
The opportunity to hunt for "treasures" lost between the cushions makes preparation for this memory game just as much fun as the game itself. Let the players lift up sofa and chair cushions and find all the "lost treasures" that have fallen down there. Some found objects just might make perfect Memory Fun game pieces for the display tray.

◆ Card Concentration ◆

2 or more players

Materials:
deck of cards

Object of the Game:
To get the most matching cards by remembering where they are after they've been turned facedown.

How to Play:
No matter what new toys or games come onto the market, a good deck of cards is always a reliable source of fun for all ages. The game of Concentration helps sharpen memory skills at the same time it beats the boredom that often is the most common cause for sibling scuffles. When fighting breaks out, break out the cards!

Shuffle the cards and place them facedown on the floor or a table. Arrange them in neat rows. Decide who goes first by turning up one card each. The highest-value card goes first. If both players choose cards of equal value, keep turning cards over until one player wins the turn.

To play the game, players take turns flipping over two cards for each turn. If a pair of matching cards is faceup, the player may take those two cards and continue playing until no match is made. Cards that do not match must be turned facedown again. Players try to concentrate on the location of the cards as they are revealed. The game continues until all the cards have been taken. The player holding the most pairs wins.

Different Ages, Different Stages:
This game can easily be simplified for younger children. Just divide the deck of cards in half or select as few as six or eight matching pairs. Siblings can play together, or side by side, using as few or as many cards as they like. The very youngest, whose attention span may be short, can be part of the game by helping

12

to lay the cards out in rows, or be in charge of holding the pairs as they are found.

Then Try This!
No cards? No problem! Let the players create their own Concentration cards. Plain index cards or even paper cut into rectangles may be decorated with drawings, letters of the alphabet, spelling words, math problems, symbols, or stickers. As long as there are two of each design, the game can be played successfully.

♦ Find It ♦
(ALL AGES)

2 or more players

Materials:
old magazines
pencil and paper for each player

Object of the Game:
To go on a scavenger hunt without leaving the house, by searching through a magazine for items on a list.

How to Play:
Sharp eyes make this scavenger hunt game a fun favorite for all ages. In the comfort of a cozy couch, kids can undertake a great search for all the items on their lists. Where will they look? In old magazines, of course!

Piles of old magazines can be reclaimed from the recycling bin and used as the "hunting ground" for the scavenger hunt. A parent or older sibling prepares for the game simply by looking through a magazine and making a list of common objects pictured within. A separate list and magazine should be given to each player. Select between ten and fifteen items to be checked off as the player finds them. Allow 15 minutes for the hunt. Players should write down the page number where each item is found. The first player to find all the items on the list wins.

Different Ages, Different Stages:
If two children of different abilities are playing this game, adjust the game appropriately. Younger children who may not be ready to write down page numbers should be given paper scraps to mark the places where items were found. To make up for age differences, make the list shorter or the hunting time longer for the younger player. For the youngest member of the group, who may not be ready for the big hunt, hand over one magazine and request that he or she find three things of a specific color. It's a good way to practice color recognition and keep the playtime peace too.

Then Try This!
Keep the magazines but change the game plan. Instead of searching for specific items, assign a letter to each player. Within a specified time limit—say, 5 minutes—players must list or mark with an *X* each item found beginning with that letter. The longest list of items wins.

◆ Eye Fooled You ◆
(AGES 3 AND UP)

2 or more players

Materials:
3 identical paper cups
small object (coin, pebble, marble, button, etc.)
timer or stopwatch
flat playing surface

Object of the Game:
To identify the cup under which the object is hidden.

How to Play:

The hand is quicker than the eye in this classic crowd pleaser. Kids of all ages (and adults too) are always ready to take the challenge of finding the hidden object under just one of the three cups. Whether a player is the finder or the cup switcher, everyone playing has to have sharp eyes.

To play there must be one player who switches the cups around on the table. The other players must try to keep their eyes on the cup under which a small object has been placed. The cup switcher begins by turning three identical cups upside down on a flat surface, placing one of the cups over the small object as he turns them over. The timer is set for 30 seconds. At the start, the cup switcher uses two hands to move all three cups around in different configurations, constantly changing their placement order on the table. The switching starts out slowly and speeds up gradually.

When the timer rings, the switching stops and each player guesses which cup hides the object. The player with the most correct guesses wins. After three games, let a new switcher take over.

Different Ages, Different Stages:

Players of the same ages will enjoy taking turns at switching cups and guessing. If older siblings are playing with much younger ones, the older player may be a faster switcher, making the game more challenging. For the very youngest sibling, who may be unable to keep up but who wants to "play," supply a pile of paper cups for building a paper cup castle or pyramid. Turned upside down, paper cups can be easily stacked and joyfully knocked down—a short distance from the cups in play, of course.

Then Try This!

If players want to play for more than just fun, make the small object under the cup be the prize for a correct guess. If a coin is used, award the coin to the winner, keeping extras on hand for more than one correct guess in a game. If candies are used, make sure they are appropriate to be eaten by the youngest player in the game.

Argument Ender #1

"You never let me win!"

If the younger sibling is unhappy because she or he can't seem to get a win, openly suggest that the elder slow down, or play a little less hard, to give the younger child a chance to score. This will allow the older child to back off a little, knowing everyone involved is aware he or she is doing so. This way, it won't be embarrassing to lose. It will also make it clear to the younger sibling that her or his request is being honored, though in a deliberate way. This younger child will feel a bit of a thrill anyway, and will likely allow the game to return to a more honest competition shortly.

◆

KITCHEN FUN

If you can't take the heat of an argument, get into the kitchen! That's the place where squabbling siblings can go to cook up some fun instead of trouble. These projects are sure to give kids food for creative thought and play.

◆ Cook's Collage ◆
(AGES 4 AND UP)

1 or more players

Materials:
white glue or paste
cotton swabs or Popsicle sticks for spreading glue
colored markers
cardboard (shirt cardboard or cut-up boxes)

16

small bowls of:
    dry cereal (Cheerios, fruit rings, etc.)
    macaroni (the more shapes the better)
    dried beans
    rice
    nuts

Object of the Project:
To create interesting designs using different textures.

How to Play:
A collage is a picture that has many different kinds of materials in it. Some collages are made using scraps of cloth, paper, wood shavings, and foil. The collage in this project is made using different foods with different textures and shapes.

Before making the collage, cover a work surface with newspaper to catch spills. Set up bowls of collage materials within easy reach of all the artists. Give each child a piece of cardboard. The artists may choose to first make an outline drawing as a guide for their gluing, or they may choose to get right to the gluing without using the markers at all. Anything goes as long as it goes on the collage surface! Decide on the type of picture or design, then use the sticks or cotton swabs to put glue on the cardboard where each collage piece will go.

Different Ages, Different Stages:
Kitchen collages can easily be a cooperative creative effort for all ages. Let siblings take turns being the glue spreaders and the materials artists. Let younger siblings create their own glue squiggle designs first. Then the older players can lay down the art materials to make the patterns they want.

Then Try This!
While the artists are in the mood to create, take the time to create a collage storage box to hold all the collage materials. Use any medium-size cardboard box. Instead of decorating the box with food items, use paper, various cloth scraps, and markers. Label the box COLLAGE KIT. Then, when the collage fun is

finished, start the collage material collection box for future fun. Store collage materials in separate airtight containers or sealable plastic bags. Keep glue and glue sticks together in a bag. Collect cardboard for "canvases." Close up the box and put it within easy reach for the next time.

◆ Apple Heads ◆
(AGES 8 AND UP)

Any number of players

Materials:
apples (1 for each head)
vegetable peeler
paring knife
warm salt water (2 cups water, 2 teaspoons salt)
beads (for eyes and teeth)
watercolor paints
colored yarn or cotton
clear glue

Object of the Project:
To make dried, shrunken apple heads. (Creepy but fun!)

How to Play:
The first thing needed is patience. While the actual carving of the apple takes only a few minutes, the drying of the apple takes about two weeks. The wait is worth it and the fun of decorating the shrunken apple heads is the best part.

First, peel a big apple. Use the paring knife to carefully carve out small areas for the eyes, nose, and mouth. Don't cut too deeply. When the apple is carved, put it in a solution of warm salt water for about 20 minutes. This keeps the apple from spoiling. Now the apple is ready for drying and shrinking. Place it in a warm, dry place. Each day it will shrink a little more. Check the apple every day and watch as it develops into a creepy-looking face. In about two weeks the apple will be ready for decorating with the finishing facial touches. Use clear glue to hold beads in place where the eyes and teeth should be. Use watercolor paints to add facial coloring—lips, eyebrows, cheek coloring. Once the paint has dried, glue on colored yarn or cotton for hair. The results? An apple head that will live "appley" ever after!

Different Ages, Different Stages:

Even the little ones can enjoy the apple-head experience if an adult does the peeling. Divide up the tasks so that everyone can take some credit for the finished apple head. Older children may do the carving. Those who are not ready to handle a knife may use a spoon instead. Little ones can measure out the salt and stir it into the warm water. Anyone can plop the apples into the salt water. And while the apple is soaking, everyone can take an apple-eating break. Two weeks later, when the apples are dried and shrunken, everyone can paint his or her own apple head.

Then Try This!

For additional fun, make a body for the apple head. Use old doll clothes stuffed with cotton or old stockings. Or make clothes out of fabric scraps. Put a stick up through the middle of the body and into the apple to attach the head. Everybody needs some body sometime, even apple heads!

◆ Taste Test ◆

(AGES 7 AND UP)

2 or more players

Materials:

2 or 3 different brands of each food for taste testing (peanut butter, chocolate milk syrups and powders, chocolate chip cookies, soft drinks, sugarless bubblegum, or any other foods that are made by different companies)

19

glass of water for each tester
paper and pencil for each tester

Object of the Game:
To identify the best foods or beverages by taste only.

How to Play:
When children are in the mood for munching, that's the perfect time to put their tongues to the test—the taste test, that is! Taste tests are fun and can also prove that what one *thinks* he or she likes best isn't always what really tastes best. Let the tongues tell the truth!

Set up the foods of your choice. For example, if peanut butter is what is being tested, select as many different brands as possible. Don't let the testers see the brands that will be tested. Give each brand a number, then take the peanut butter out of the jars and put each kind in a separate bowl. Number the bowls to match the jars from which they were filled. Put a separate spreading knife in each bowl so flavors won't get mixed.

Give each tester paper and a pencil for grading and for comments. Give each tester a glass of water for rinsing the mouth between tastes. As the testers sample each brand, they should write down the number of the peanut butter and any comments so they can remember what they thought when it comes to final grading. After the tasting is finished, testers should read over their comments and decide on a final grade for each brand: A for "Absolutely Fabulous"; B for "Better than Average"; C for "Could Be Better"; D for "Don't Spread This on My Bread!"; and F for "Food Flop." Give 20 points for each A, 15 points for each B, 10 points for each C, 5 points for each D, and 0 points for each F. The peanut butter with the most points wins.

Different Ages, Different Stages:
While this activity is fun for anyone with a tongue and taste buds, young siblings who can't write or add up number scores can still be included. In fact, the more testers the better. Children of all ages have opinions. Younger children can work

along with the older ones, letting the older brother or sister record grades and comments. Even the youngest peanut butter tasters can yell out "Bad," "Okay," or "Great" after each spoonful of peanut butter is tasted. An older sibling can record the comments of the younger ones.

Then Try This!
Leftover peanut butter need not be wasted. See "For the Birds," in chapter 4, to find out how to make a peanut butter–covered pinecone bird feeder.

◆ Snack Attack Invention ◆

(AGES 4 AND UP)

Any number of players

Materials:
edible ingredients (peanut butter, apples, bananas, honey, coconut, cream cheese, celery, carrots, raisins, nuts, yogurt, frozen yogurt, granola, or any other healthful foods)
measuring spoons
measuring cup
mixing bowls (if necessary)
bowls for each ingredient
plate for each inventor
utensils for spreading and eating
paper and pencil for writing down recipes

Object of the Project:
To invent and name a new and healthful snack.

How to Play:
Snack time is a great time for teaching kids how to create their own snacks. Allow them to select ingredients that are considered nutritious. Flavor favorites are sure to be found when the ingredients are mixed and matched with the inventor's taste buds in mind.

Have all the Snack Attack inventors wash their hands before starting. Give each inventor space in which to work. Provide a pencil and paper so the inventor can keep track of quantities of ingredients used as recipes are tried. Set up the Snack Attack Invention counter with bowls of various ingredients. A parent or older sibling should do any peeling and slicing of fruit. Quantities should be kept small until the invented snack has passed the taste-bud test. Encourage experimentation with flavors and food textures. Allow the inventors to taste one another's experiments. When the best recipes have been found, write down the exact measurements for each recipe and have the inventor give the new snack sensation a name. Inventors may share their recipes for future snack times. And while the sharing mood is there, share the clean-up duties too!

Different Ages, Different Stages:
While the older siblings are doing the real snack inventing, let the younger inventors in on the fun too. Make them the designated sprinklers and spreaders, allowing them to help without hindering. Make a work space for them that is low enough for them to reach it easily and safely.

Then Try This!
Healthful food may usually be a parent's first choice in snacking, but special occasions call for special treats. Turn the Snack Attack Invention time into a Make-Your-Own-Ice-Cream Sundae time. Fill bowls with one scoop of ice cream. Then let the inventors spoon on their own toppings from a selection set out in bowls on a counter. Some topping suggestions are: sprinkles, gumdrops, crushed cookies, chocolate syrup, butterscotch syrup, nuts, whipped cream, and cherries. Inventors' eyes may be bigger than their stomachs, but the fun is in the creating. This idea makes a party even more special for all ages.

♦ Organize Everything ♦

1 or more players

Materials:
things to be organized and sorted (coupons, soups, spices, cereals, pots and pans, pantry closet shelves, etc.)

Object of the Project:
To learn to organize, alphabetize, and tidy up while having fun.

How to Play:
Neatness counts in this cozy kitchen activity. In fact, neatness is the activity. Everyone can "play" and in the end the kitchen will be the tidiest room in the house.

Organization is the name of the game, and here are the things to assign to the organizers:

• *Canned Soups*—Older kids can alphabetize and order the soups in the cabinet. Start with the Alphabet Soup and don't stop until you stack the last can of Zucchini with Rice. Younger kids can just sort through the canned foods and organize all the soups in one section of a shelf.

• *Spices*—As with the soups, let older kids alphabetize and order the spices in the cabinet. As they put the jars in order, let them read each label to find out what uses each spice has. Younger kids can simply order the jars by size.

• *Pots and Pans*—Any age can stack the pots and pans inside one another. Put the pot tops in size order inside a big pot. No banging the pots, please. Remember, someone may be sleeping!

• *Coupons*—Let the kids do the coupon clipping, sorting, and saving. Starting with the Sunday newspaper, allow those handy with scissors to go through the coupon sections and clip the coupons for products your family really uses. Order them according to where the products are in the aisles of the supermarket, or just in product similarity groups—all the cereal coupons together, all the ones for household cleaning products

23

together, and so forth. Older kids can add up the savings to find out the real cash value of their efforts.

Different Ages, Different Stages:
Give the littlest organizers a low shelf of their own to organize however they like. Stock it with different sizes of canned foods, boxes of dried foods, and a couple of pots and pans. While the older sibling organizes the family shelves, the younger one can organize his or her own shelf. As big brother or big sister places items in order, he or she may take the opportunity to show the younger one how things may be organized by size, shape, and color.

Then Try This!
While organizers are working, they can also play Alphabet Scavenger Hunt. The object of the game is to find as many letters of the alphabet as possible just on soup names, spice names, or cereal names. The first one to find the letters *A* to *Z* wins.

◆ Chapter 3 ◆

It's Raining, It's Pouring, and Life's Getting Boring

Stuck-in-the-House Fun

DON'T LET RAIN throw a wet blanket on your children's play day. Bad moods triggered by bad weather can be cleared up fast with the help of some quick and easy activities. There's always fun to be found if you take a few minutes to make a few game plans. Here are some welcome alternatives to television that children will like tuning into again and again.

BOREDOM BEATERS

Give boredom the boot with this handful of helpful make-and-do boredom beaters. The supplies needed for each activity are things commonly found around most homes. Next time outside is off-limits for play, turn the inside into a place full of fun things to do. Even if the sun doesn't come out, the smiles will!

◆ Making Bubbles ◆

1 or more players

Materials:

For bubbles solution:
   bowl or wide-mouth jar
   $\frac{1}{2}$ cup liquid detergent
   $\frac{1}{2}$ cup water
   $\frac{1}{8}$ tsp. sugar
For bubble blowers:
   straws
   paper clips

Object of the Project:

To create bubbles just for fun.

How to Play:

Bubbles make people happy. Even the word *bubbles* has a giggly sound to it. Watching a rainbow-colored bubble float through the air until it meets its squeaky-pop end is a simple pleasure that can be created easily. Bubbles may be blown in the kitchen, laundry area, or playroom without worry. The soapy solution is harmless to furnishings and may be easily wiped off tile floors.

First, make the bubble solution by mixing equal amounts of liquid detergent and water. This recipe calls for $\frac{1}{2}$ cup of each plus $\frac{1}{8}$ teaspoon of sugar. Stir the solution until it is thoroughly mixed.

Second, make a bubble blower. If a straw is used, make a small slit in one side at one end. Fold back the straw along the slit (see illustration). Dip the slit end of the straw into the bubble solution. Blow lightly through the other end of the straw.

If a paper clip is used, unbend it and reshape it into a ring with a handle. Dip the ring into the bubble solution and blow lightly.

Bubble Blower

Different Ages, Different Stages:
Divide up the bubble-making duties so that older children do the measuring of the liquids and the making of the bubble blowers. The younger siblings can do the stirring. And everyone can blow bubbles. Even the littlest toddlers delight in trying to catch a bubble.

Then Try This!
"Bobby blew blue bubbles. Bobby blew blue bubbles. Bobby blew blue bubbles." Say it fast three times and listen as the giggles add an extra bit of bubbly fun to the bubble blowing.

◆ Play Dough ◆

1 or more players

Materials:
large bowl
wooden spoon
measuring cup
1½ cups flour
½ cup salt
¼ cup water (added slowly)
¼ cup vegetable oil (added slowly)
optional: food coloring (added to water)

Object of the Project:
To mix up a batch of play dough and create some craft fun.

How to Play:
Why buy the claylike substance Play-Doh, when it's so easy to make at home? Kids of all ages can mix up a batch of it in a jiffy, and once they've made it the play dough play can go on for hours.

In the large bowl, mix the 1½ cups of flour and the ½ cup of salt. Slowly stir in the ¼ cup of water, then slowly stir in the ¼ cup of vegetable oil. If the players want the play dough to have a color, add a couple of drops of food coloring to the water before adding the water to the mixture. Use the spoon to mix the dough until all the flour and salt are moistened. Then hands may do the kneading until the dough is the desired consistency.

When the dough is done, the playing fun begins. Suggest any or all of the following play ideas:

1. Make play dough food for a doll and stuffed animal dinner party.
2. Create play dough sculptures.

3. Use cookie cutters to make play dough cookie shapes.
4. Have a Guess What? contest. Each play dough player makes something and the other player must guess what it is.
5. Make play dough snakes by rolling balls of it in the palms of the hands.
6. Make play dough pottery. First make a flat bottom of play dough. Build up the sides with play dough shakes curled around the bottom and stacked on top of each other. Or just shape vases, bowls, jars, plates, and cups with play dough.

Play dough can be saved for several weeks if stored in a tightly closed plastic bag kept in the refrigerator. If the dough dries out a little bit, pat a small amount of vegetable oil on the outside of it.

Different Ages, Different Stages:
Play dough play has its appeal for all ages. The older the player, the more sophisticated the creations may be. Let the older children do the measuring and the younger ones do the stirring. Older children can let their imaginations run free, creating "let's pretend" games for the younger ones (for example, "Let's pretend it's real food," "Let's pretend we're making dollhouse furniture." "Let's pretend we're making a play dough zoo").

Then Try This!
Make play dough holiday ornaments. Put a hole in the top of the design. Allow it to dry thoroughly. Paint with poster paints. Add a ribbon for hanging. (Hint: For faster drying, an adult may help by putting the ornaments on a tray in a toaster oven and baking at 350° until dry, or about 10 minutes.)

◆ Finger Puppets ◆

2 or more players

Materials:
fingers
fine-point, washable, colored felt-tipped pens

Object of the Project:
To create finger puppets and finger-puppet shows.

How to Play:
There's a world of entertainment right at your fingertips. All it takes to get a handle on the puppet-show fun is a hand full of fingers, some marking pens, and a willingness to have some silly fun. Three different types of puppets can be made from one simple hand. It's a giggle-getting thing to do. Try it!

• *Puppet 1, Fingers only:* Holding the hand up so that all five fingers are spread apart and pointing up, turn the hand so that the palm side will be the drawing surface. Draw tiny facial features on each finger. Add hair and clothes (see illustration). When the finger puppets are finished and ready to wiggle until the audience giggles, make the finger puppets talk. A simple "Hello, I am not an actor. I am a real finger talking to you" is sure to get a giggle from any finger-puppet fan!

• *Puppet 2, Fist only:* Make a loose fist with the thumb bent and tucked under the index finger. Before drawing the face on the hand, practice moving the thumb up and down as a lower lip of a mouth might move. Draw lips around the opening. Draw eyes and a nose on the index finger knuckle that is sticking up (see illustration). This talking hand will always get a laugh even if it only looks someone in the face, opens its mouth, and says "Boo!"

Finger Puppet 1

Finger Puppet 2

•*Puppet 3, Whole Hand:* For hand-puppet designers who want to make their puppets walk and talk, the whole hand may be used. Just fold in the thumb, pinky, and ring finger. Turn the hand upside down and think of the index and middle fingers as the legs (see illustration). Draw clothes and the upper part of a body above the middle joints. Some suggestions for characters are a ballet dancer, a bird with long legs, a clown, or a silly monster. This handy puppet doesn't have to say a word to get the audience laughing. Just a few kicks of the legs will do the giggle-getting trick!

Finger Puppet 3

Different Ages, Different Stages:
There's no age limit for finger-puppet fun. The smaller the fingers, the smaller the puppets, but any size gets a giggle. Older siblings can do the drawing on the fingers and hands of the younger ones. Let the youngest children choose the colors to be used.

Then Try This!
Bring finger puppets along on any car trip or restaurant outing. They are the easiest take-along entertainment center available!

◆ Disguise the Limit ◆

(AGES 3 AND UP)

Any number of players

Materials:

white glue	egg cartons
tape	straws
scissors	Styrofoam packing pieces
hole puncher	feathers
markers, crayons, colored	cotton balls
pencils	yarn
paper plates	old stockings
construction paper	aluminum foil
paper bags (all sizes)	string

Object of the Project:
To create disguises for all occasions—Halloween, costume parties, or days when kids feel like changing their looks.

How to Play:
Face it. Sometimes the face in the mirror needs a little livening up. Disguises are just the thing when the same old face needs a lift.

Start the disguise play by gathering all the tools and materials needed. If everything has already been collected in a supply box, you're one step ahead of the game. Decide if you will make a mask or a whole head covering.

Paper plates used whole or cut in half make great full-face masks, half masks, or goggle-type masks (see illustration). A hole punched at each edge of the plate and string tied through each hole holds the mask in place. Cut eyeholes and spaces for nose and mouth. Decorate the plates simply with markers, or use white glue to attach other materials.

Paper bags may be used as whole head coverings. Cut eye, nose, and mouth holes. Cut a curved shape on both sides of the bag where it meets the shoulders. Decorate the bag with markers or glue on other materials (see illustration).

Suggestions for masks are clown, astronaut, space alien, monster, beautiful lady, animal.

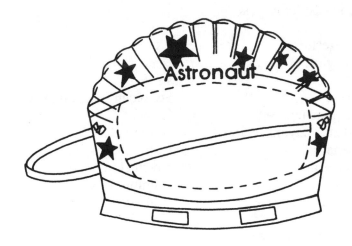

Paper Plate Mask

Different Ages, Different Stages:

Halloween and class plays may be the times when older children most enjoy the fun of creating disguises. Older children may see the activity as "babyish" unless it is done with a specific purpose in mind. However, the presence of younger siblings in a household gives older siblings additional opportunity to participate in the fun of "playing" with disguises just for the fun of it. Let the older children help the younger ones design and create their masks. Older siblings may make masks of their own just to show the younger ones how to do it. In the role of "teacher," older siblings can still have fun and not feel they are doing something inappropriate for their age group.

Paper Bag Mask

Then Try This!
Masks are not just child's play. They are an art form with historical significance in theater and in different cultures. The art section of the library will offer a serious look at masks and may give children some ideas for more sophisticated creations.

Argument Ender #2

"But he won't let me do it that way!"

You've given instructions to both your children. The older one does it this way, the younger one that way. It worked for a while but now the younger child wants to do it the "big" way and your elder is saying "You can't! You're too little!" Step in and say to the younger, "Okay, why don't you give it a try?" Then tell both children if it doesn't work they'll both go back to the original plan. Stand there and watch so that it isn't left to the older to make the judgment call. If your younger child really can't pull it off, help him or her save face by changing the original role or task just a little bit. If it's a question of starting lines, move the younger child's up just a little. If it's a question of manual skills, suggest the younger child cut out only the last piece of decoration instead of all of them.

◆

◆ Aye, That's the Rub ◆
(AGES 3 AND UP)

1 or more players

Materials:
paper
crayon or soft lead pencil

36

textured items (coins, embossed credit cards, leaves, soles of shoes, a straw mat, string, etc.)

Object of the Project:
To make designs called "rubbings."

How to Play:
The art form known as "rubbing" is easily done and produces some beautiful designs. Some people make rubbings of tombstones, plaques on buildings or monuments, and brass plates used for printmaking. Equally beautiful rubbings can be made at home using objects found around the house. The process is simple.

Start with a coin. Lay the coin on a hard, flat surface. Cover it with a piece of paper. Using the side of a pencil point or crayon, rub gently back and forth over the coin. Immediately you will see the raised parts of the coin being shaded and showing up on the paper. Make the rubbing light or dark. Try it again using different colored pencils or crayons.

Different Ages, Different Stages:
Younger children may need to be reminded not to press too hard, in order to avoid tearing the paper. They may also be encouraged to color in their finished rubbings if they like.

Older children should be encouraged to think of other possible subjects that may be found inside or outside the house. Some suggestions are: carvings on a picture frame or molding, old radiator covers or vent covers, your car's license plate, the numbers on your mailbox, a tree trunk, and different flat stones. Discovering that almost all things have different textures and patterns is fun.

Then Try This!
A trip to a cemetery may sound like a gloomy affair, but in fact it can be extremely interesting when done with rubbings in mind. With permission from the groundskeeper, there are many beautiful rubbings to be made. Bring a supply of larger paper and perhaps some special silver and gold flat crayons made especially for rubbings and sold in art stores.

◆ Music, Music, Music ◆

1 or more players

Materials:

To make a xylophone you will need:
  6 empty glass soda bottles
  water
  spoon or fork
To make a one-note dooty-doot-doot you will need:
  paper
  scissors
To make a pair of shakers you will need:
  2 empty round salt cartons
  dried beans or rice
  tape
  2 sticks (at least 10 inches long)

Object of the Project:

To make musical instruments out of ordinary household items.

How to Play:

The house can be just as alive with the sound of music as the hills. Making musical instruments is easy and fun. Make one or all of the instruments here, then let the music begin.

• *Xylophone*—Use six bottles of the same shape and size. Fill one bottle almost all the way to the top. Fill another one two thirds of the way. Fill the third one halfway, and fill the last three with different amounts. Line them up and tap each one lightly with the kitchen utensil of your choice. To change the sounds, change the amounts of water.

• *Dooty-Doot-Doot*—Cut a piece of paper into a rectangle six inches long and three inches wide. Fold the paper in half. Fold up each end about half an inch (see illustration). In the middle of where the paper is folded, cut out a *V*-shape about half an inch wide. Hold out your index finger and middle finger in a scissorlike position. Hold the paper between the fingers and bring the two folded ends up to your lips. Now just blow and listen to the one-note dooty-doot-doot sound.

• *Shakers*—Pour dried beans or rice into the spout of the salt carton. Tape the spout closed. Mark the center of each end of each carton. Push a stick through each mark so that it pokes out two inches on one end, with the rest to be used as a handle. Secure the sticks in place by putting tape around where the stick pokes through. Hold one in each hand and shake!

Different Ages, Different Stages:
Children who are too young to make these musical instruments will have fun dancing and playing to the sounds of the music made by older siblings. Older children can make instruments for the younger ones to decorate with crayons and markers. Even the youngest musicians can shake the shakers while older musicians perhaps play real instruments such as a recorder, piano, or guitar. Suggest that younger children play along with one of their music tapes or records. The older children can use their instruments to cheer on their school soccer teams, make

One-Note Dooty-Doot-Doot

39

their presence known at a holiday party, or just cheer up the neighborhood.

Then Try This!

Build the band into an orchestra. Let the musicians experiment by making other instruments. A rubber band stretched over a paper cup from bottom to top can be pulled and plucked for a great banjo sound. Tissue paper around a comb can be hummed into, and the sound is as funny as the feeling on the lips. The house is full of musical possibilities.

CONTEST TIME

Contest games are the kind found at fairs and carnivals where hand-eye coordination is tested at booth after booth. Such games offer a challenge beyond just winning or losing. A test of a specific skill may also be part of the play. In these games good aim is an important skill. But no matter how good their throwing aim, children who aim to have fun are sure to hit the bull's-eye every time!

◆ Sunken Treasure ◆
(AGES 4 AND UP)

2 or more players

Materials:
large wide-mouth container
small jar or glass
water
5 coins per player
3 extra coins for tiebreakers

Object of the Game:
To try to get the most coins into the small jar or glass.

How to Play:
Fill the large-mouth container with water. Sink the small jar or glass in the middle. Put the container on the floor. Decide who goes first by flipping one of the coins and calling heads or tails. Heads wins the turn. One at a time, each player stands over the container and tries to drop his or her five coins into the small jar or glass. Keep score of how many coins go into the center container. A tie may be broken with the last tiebreaker coins. The player who gets the most coins into the jar or glass wins and may keep all the coins around the center jar. Those coins in the center jar or glass go to the runner-up.

Different Ages, Different Stages:
Older children may have steadier hands and better aim, but young children may be shorter and closer to the target. However, if an adjustment for fairness must be made, allow the younger player more coins and more chances to get one in the small jar. Younger children may also be encouraged to practice counting and coin identification. Use pennies, nickels, and dimes instead of only pennies. Encourage the older players to practice addition using the coin values. Add up how much money is in the small jar and how much is around it.

Then Try This!
Add variety to the game by changing the placement of the jars. Place two small jars side by side in a washtub filled with water. Or eliminate the importance of good aim by covering the bottom of a water-filled container with many jars and letting the penny pitching be more random.

Play the game for UNICEF or some other worthy charity. Instead of keeping the coins, have the children donate them to a cause in which they believe. Take the opportunity to discuss environmental causes and social causes, explaining how even a few cents donated by many people can make a difference.

◆ Fish and Clips ◆

2 or more players

Materials:
paper clips
paper fish cut out of construction paper
cardboard box with high sides
magnet on a string

Object of the Game:
To catch as many "fish" on the magnet as possible.

How to Play:
Clip one paper clip onto each fish. The magnet on the string is the fishhook. Drop the paper-clipped fish into the big cardboard box. Spread the fish around on the bottom of the box so they're not all clumped together. Place the big box in the middle of a table, high enough so the players cannot see into it.

The first player drops the magnet on the string into the box and moves it around to catch as many fish as possible. Set a timer for 30 seconds for each turn. When the time is up, the player pulls up the "hook" to see how many fish have been caught. Remove them, count them, and throw them back into the box. The next player takes a turn, and so on until everyone has had at least one turn. If only two are playing, set a time limit for each game and play best three out of five games. Keep a written score for each player. The one with the most fish caught wins.

Different Ages, Different Stages:
Add an extra challenge for older players by raising the height of the box, placing fewer fish in the box, and spreading them out more. To give younger players an extra advantage, allow them to look into the box when they are fishing.

42

Then Try This!
Fish for found objects instead. Assign different point values to such metal objects as bobby pins, safety pins, and paper clips. Let the players fish for points. The player with the most points wins.

Argument Ender #3

"He always wins! I hate him!"

Losing is never easy. Disappointment in one's own performance can cause one sibling to look for a target. Usually it's the sibling who won the game. Saying "I hate you!" is sometimes the first dart to be thrown. A parent needs to help both siblings understand what's going on. To the loser one might say, "This is a hard game and losing feels bad. It can even make you feel hateful. You are good enough to win, but this time it was your brother's turn to win. Perhaps you'll win the next game."

The winner also needs to hear from the mediator. "Congratulations on winning a hard game. You must feel happy to be the one who won this time. Maybe you could teach your brother some tricks so he can win a few too!"

◆ Moon Rock Roll ◆
(AGES 4 AND UP)

2 or more players

Materials:
5 cotton balls per player
string to mark the start and finish lines

Object of the Game:

To move all the "moon rocks" from the start line to the finish line by blowing on them.

How to Play:

What's the surest way to lose weight? Go to the moon! On the moon everything is weightless. Even the moon rocks. In this game, cotton balls are the "moon rocks" that must be moved from start to finish by the players. Sounds easy, right? But there is one catch to it: the players must be on their hands and knees and may move the "rocks" only by blowing on them.

Stretch out a string where the players will start. Leave enough room between the players so they don't bump into each other during the race. At the opposite end of the play area, no more than ten feet from the start, stretch another piece of string out to mark the finish line.

Each player is given five "moon rocks" to move, one at a time. As one "moon rock" is blown to the finish line, the player returns to the start line and blows another "rock" down the line until all five are moved. The first player to move all five is the winner.

Different Ages, Different Stages:

This game is easily adapted to any age. To simplify it for younger children who may be short of breath or lack energy for crawling, shorten the distance between the start and finish lines and/or give each player only one or two cotton balls to move.

Then Try This!

When hands and knees get tired of crawling, play the game in an upright position. Give each player a drinking straw and one cotton ball. Instead of blowing, the player must suck in through the straw and try to hold the cotton ball on the end of it while moving from the start to the finish. The player who reaches the farthest point is the winner.

◆ Ice Capades ◆

2 or more players

Materials:
2 drinking straws per player
2 bowls of warm water
1 ice cube per player

Object of the Game:
To pick up the ice cube with straw "chopsticks" before it melts.

How to Play:
This game is a race against the time it takes for an ice cube to melt. It is played by two players at a time, and may be played with teams or just with one against one.

Provide each player with a pair of drinking straws, which will be held in only one hand as chopsticks. Set up two bowls of warm water. Have each player stand in front of a bowl with chopsticks ready. On the word "Start" an ice cube is dropped into each bowl. The players must then try to catch the ice cube in their chopsticks and remove it from the warm water before it melts. The winner is the player who removes the biggest lump of ice. Be sure to change the water after each set of players so that it stays warm even for the last set of players.

Different Ages, Different Stages:
Holding two straws in one hand may be too difficult for smaller hands. If this proves to be the case, allow younger players to hold one straw in each hand. If there is a big difference between ages of players, make the water cooler for the youngest player so the ice lasts longer or make the older player's water warmer.

Then Try This!
Add an extra element of fun to the game by preparing prize ice cubes ahead of time. Fill an ice cube tray with water and drop

a penny, a charm, or a cherry into each cube compartment. Freeze the tray and watch the delight on the players' faces when even a melted ice cube offers a consolation prize.

Argument Ender #4

"That's not fair!"

Take the charge out of the argument by acknowledging that both players are part of the disagreement: "You both feel you are right. If you cannot come to an agreement the game will probably be over. I think you can still have fun if you would agree to trust each other." Encourage them to discuss what didn't seem fair and to establish a clear rule so that what's "fair" will not be open to interpretation. Then suggest they either redo the last "move" or begin again.

◆

◆ Two Can Play ◆
(AGES 5 TO 8)

2 or more players

Materials:
6 soup or juice cans (washed and checked for smooth rims)
old magazines or comics
scissors
white glue
2 paint brushes or Q-tips to spread glue
6 pennies
pencil and paper for scoring

Object of the Game:

To decorate containers to be used in a penny pitch game. In the game the object is to gather points by tossing pennies into the cans. The one with the most points wins.

Craft Fun:

Each child has three cans to decorate. Art is in the eye of the beholder, so there is no right or wrong in the creation of it. This should be made clear to all children playing. Make the job worry-free by first covering the work space with newspaper. Assign different jobs to each artist. The older one may be better at handling scissors. Let him or her cut out the pictures, comic characters from old magazines and newspapers, or just shapes cut from colored construction paper. Spreading glue is easy for all ages. Let the younger child prepare the cans with glue while big brother or sister is doing the scissor work. Using a brush or a Q-tip, spread glue over the outside of the can being decorated. Once the cans are covered with glue, both children may do the decorating at the same time. Place pictures or comics over the glue. Continue until the can is completely covered. When all six cans have been decorated, there's no need to wait for them to dry. Let the game begin!

How to Play:

Whether you're rushing to make a meal or a meeting, the children can make it easier by playing together pleasantly and peacefully like friends rather than siblings. No matter what the age difference between them, the enjoyment will be the same as they work together and at their own individual levels to create can art that can be used for a game called Grand Can Penny Pitch.

Arrange the cans in three rows forming a triangle—three cans in the front row, two in the second row, one in the last row. Set the cans equal distances apart, and set the rules so that all is fair according to varying abilities of the different ages.

Each penny landing in a front-row can equals one point. The second row of cans equals two points. The third row equals three points.

Decide who goes first by flipping one of the pennies and calling heads or tails. Each turn allows a player to toss six pennies. A fair tossing distance from the cans can be determined by having each player stand directly in front of the first row of cans and step back four steps equal to the size of his or her foot. Standing behind an imaginary line four "my own feet" away from the cans, the first player tosses pennies to the cans. After each turn is completed, add up the points and take the pennies out of the cans for the next player's turn. The first player to earn ten points wins the game.

Then Try This!

When the game is over, suggest that the works of can art be wrapped up and given as pencil holders to grandparents or other relatives who would appreciate receiving an original piece of art for a birthday or holiday gift.

GIGGLE GETTERS

Some fun just has a way of getting the giggles going. Here are some games that are long on laughs, short on difficulty, and just right for those days when it's too hot, too cold, or too wet to go outside.

◆ Ha Ha ◆

(ALL AGES)

2 or more players

Materials:

none needed

Object of the Game:

To keep a straight face while other players try to make you laugh.

How to Play:

When the cousins come for a visit and the siblings pair off with their favorite, ganging up on each other can be a problem. This fun and funny game gets the giggles going in everyone. No one is too young or too old to laugh, and Ha Ha proves it!

Lie down on the floor. If only two players are playing, Player 1 lies with head on the floor. Player 2 lies with his or her head on Player 1's stomach. If three or more players play, each player's head should rest on another player's stomach. One player begins by simply saying "Ha!" The next player continues with "Ha ha!"

The next player follows with "Ha ha ha!" and so on, with each turn adding another "ha." Of course, all of the Ha-ha-ing must be done with a straight face. Impossible? Yes! And when a player cracks up he or she is out. That player may continue to try to make the other players laugh, but no touching is allowed. The player to keep the straightest face longest wins the game. However, everyone wins a good laugh!

Different Ages, Different Stages:

Little players may not be able to hold in their laughter long enough to make the game last. Give them the advantage of starting over three times before they are out.

Then Try This!

Keep the ha-ha's going with additional giggle-getting fun.

• *Joke Telling*—Players take turns telling jokes with heads still on stomachs, trying to make the other player(s) laugh.

• *Make a Funny Face*—Players try to make one another laugh with the funniest faces possible—and facing one another, of course.

• *Staring Contest*—Players look into one another's eyes as long as possible. The first one to laugh loses.

◆ Camouflage ◆

2 or more players

Materials:
items to be hidden (coin, key, stamp, paper clip, teabag, button,
    piece of jewelry, small toy, safety pin, barrette, etc.)
pencil for each player
list of items for each player

Object of the Game:
To be the first to find all the objects, which are hidden in plain
sight but camouflaged.

How to Play:
Someone who is not playing in the game must be the one to
hide ten objects. The trick in hiding items is to find hiding
places that are in plain sight but that camouflage the item being hidden. For example, a hairpin hidden on a fire screen is
almost impossible to see, but it's right there in plain sight.
When all the items have been hidden, each player is given a
list of the items and a pencil to use to check off items as they
are spotted. Each player hunts quietly for the items. When
an item is spotted, the player checks the item off on the list
and tries not to give any sign of the sighting to other players.
The first player to check off all the items on the list is the
winner.

Different Ages, Different Stages:
Younger children who can't read yet may be included in the
game if an older child helps read the list. Or, the game can be
simplified for younger players by drawing pictures of the items
for the list instead of writing out the words.

Then Try This!
A hunt is always a fun activity for all ages. A roll of pennies
hidden around the house provides a good game any time. Hide

the loose pennies under sofa cushions, in drawers, in corners, on windowsills, and anywhere else. The player who finds the most pennies is the winner.

◆ Nose Knows ◆

(ALL AGES)

2 or more players

Materials:
10 empty containers
10 different-smelling items (vinegar, vanilla extract, mustard, lemon juice, perfume, coffee, peanut butter, chocolate sauce, water, etc.)
pencil and paper for each player
paper and tape to cover jars
blindfold for each player

Object of the Game:
To correctly identify the contents of the jars by scent alone.

How to Play:
Put a small amount of each item in separate containers. Cover the containers with paper to hide the contents. Number the containers from one to ten. Give each player a paper with the numbers one to ten written on it. Blindfold each player as he or she smells the contents of each container. When a player has finished smelling the contents of a container, the blindfold may be removed, and the player may write the guessed identity of the container's contents next to the corresponding number on the paper. The blindfold must be put back on for each jar so that there is no peeking. The player whose nose knows the most is the winner.

Different Ages, Different Stages:
Younger players may not be familiar with as many scents as older players. At the same time that the older players are guess-

ing scents, arrange a different set of scents specifically familiar to the younger players. If they are not able to write down their guesses, an older sibling may help. Some possible scents that are more familiar to younger noses are: apple juice, peanut butter, chocolate syrup, orange juice, and a parent's cologne.

Then Try This!

While the nose is being tested, try this scientific experiment to discover how closely the sense of smell works with the sense of taste. Cut one small piece of onion and one thin slice of apple, both about the same size. Blindfold one sibling and say, "Hold your nose and breathe through your mouth. Stick out your tongue." Let the other sibling place either the piece of onion or the piece of apple on the blindfolded sibling's tongue. Say to the blindfolded sibling, "Pull your tongue into your mouth but don't chew. Keep holding your nose." Ask him or her to identify which food is on the tongue. It will not be possible. Then say, "Let go of your nose and sniff deeply. Now can you tell me which food is on your tongue?" Sense of taste needs sense of smell to correctly identify a food item.

◆ Creepy Feelies ◆

(AGES 3 AND UP)

2 or more players

Materials:

1 big bowl filled with the following items:
cold cooked spaghetti for worms, peeled grapes for eyeballs, dried apricots for ears, almonds for witch's teeth, and fat pretzel sticks for bones
1 big bowl of soapy water for a "pool of acid"
paper towels

Object of the Game:

To get the giggles just by feeling creepy things in the dark.

How to Play:

This completely creepy game is guaranteed to give players the giggles as well as the creeps.

Prepare the bowl of creepy things ahead of time. Don't let the players see the bowl until it's game time. Have the players sit down on the floor. Turn the lights down low or blindfold the players. Start the fun with a creepy story about being lost in a witch's castle where no lights are on. The only way to get through the creepy place is to catch the witch with one of her own creepy spells. The ingredients for the spell are all in the bowl. Players must find each ingredient by touch alone. Pass the bowl around, and instruct each player to find a specific ingredient—say, one eyeball, three worms, two ears, a bone from a witch's finger, four teeth from a toothless witch. Along with the giggles there may be some howls, squeals, and screeches. It's all for fun and it ends with the last bowl—the pool of cool acid—which is actually soapy water just right for clean-up. Pass the paper towels around at the end and congratulate the players on surviving the creepiest Creepy Feelies game ever played.

Different Ages, Different Stages:

Young children may find this whole idea a little too frightening to play with the lights out. Keep the lights on for them and before the game begins pass around a bowl of "antispell pills" to keep them safe from all witches. The "pills" can actually be candies or raisins. If younger children don't want to participate, let them in on the secret of the "secret ingredients" and they'll get the giggles too as they watch their older siblings being fooled. Let the young ones help set the mood by adding some spooky "Oooooooooo"'s and some creepy-sounding cackling.

Then Try This!

If the creepiness of this disturbs anyone, change the way it's played. Let the players create their own ideas for what the bowls of things might contain. Let their imaginations go wild and see what happens.

Argument Ender #5

"She's cheating!"

Is she? Intentional cheating is never allowed. If a sibling has peeked when she shouldn't have peeked, moved when he shouldn't have moved, or somehow altered his own or another player's score, this is cheating. However, if a finish line is moved closer or requirements for winning a game are adapted to be age-appropriate, this is not cheating . . . though the other player may interpret it as such, even if you go to great pains to explain what you are doing before the games begin! A simple reminder, such as "When you were four years old and playing this game, we did the same for you," or "She would very much like to be as big as you are (or as old, or as experienced), but until she is, the game must be made fair for her as well," should do nicely.

◆

◆ Chapter 4 ◆

Outside, Rarin' to Go

Getting Along with One Another
and Nature

OPEN THE DOORS, let the sunshine in, and let the children out! On days when the weather invites everyone to come out and play, knowing just *what* to play can be a problem. This full-of-fun section offers activity ideas to help siblings make the most of days too beautiful to waste squabbling.

NATURE FUN

Nature is a natural when it comes to filling a sunny day with a wealth of healthful activities. Signs and sounds of nature are everywhere—in the city, in the suburbs, and in the country. Here are some playful ways to take advantage of all it has to offer.

◆ The Hole Thing ◆

1 or more players

Materials:
shovel and other digging tools for each player
Optional: small toy cars and trucks

Object of the Game:
To dig and discover the joys of playing in the dirt.

How to Play:
There's something about a hole in the ground that fascinates kids. New treasures may be buried in them. Old treasures may be found in them. Holes are made to be dug or filled, and digging is an activity kids can really get into.

Find a spot in the yard where a hole may be dug safely and inconspicuously. Give each player a digging tool and the freedom to dig in the designated area. Suggest the following digging activities:

- Create a maze of dirt roads and tunnels for toy cars and trucks to run through.
- Have a hole-digging contest—whoever digs the deepest hole in three minutes is the winner.
- Have a buried-treasure hunt—each player buries a "treasure," such as a small toy car, for the other player(s) to find.
- Dig a hole for a fort or club meeting place.

Different Ages, Different Stages:
While younger children may enjoy digging just for the pure joy of it, older children may need to dig with a purpose. Provide a packet of flower seeds and let the older diggers plant them according to the package instructions.

Then Try This!

Once a hole is dug, fill it with a family time capsule to be dug up at a much later date. To make the time capsule, fill a mayonnaise jar or other large jar with personal family mementos— recent photos; notes giving each person's name, age, and the date the capsule is filled; ticket stubs from a recent special event; a list of each person's favorite color, television show, song, singing group, book, and sports teams. Seal the jar tightly and bury it in the hole. Be sure to mark the burial spot clearly so it can be found in the future. Mark your calendar with a reminder to mark the next year's calendar with another reminder. Even a year later, the time capsule will be fun to unearth and examine.

◆ For the Birds ◆

(AGES 3 AND UP)

1 or more players

Materials:
pinecone
peanut butter
birdseed
hanging wire or string
an orange or grapefruit
popcorn
needle and thread
pencil and paper for each player
bird book for identification purposes

Object of the Project:
To make a variety of bird feeders, and then to track the numbers and kinds of birds that eat from them.

How to Play:

This project/game may be for the birds, but it's also for everyone to enjoy. Once the easy bird feeders are made, the whole family will be bird-watching.

To start, make just one—or make all—of the bird feeders described here. Let the younger siblings work on the easiest two, listed first, while the older children work on the more difficult one.

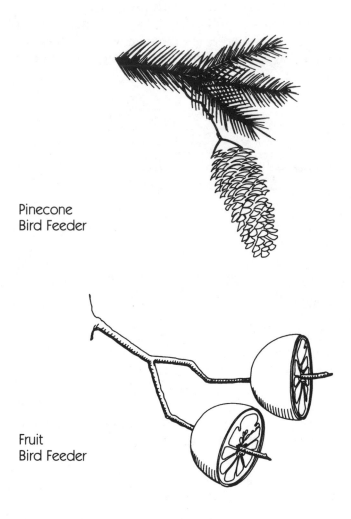

Pinecone
Bird Feeder

Fruit
Bird Feeder

• *Pinecone Feeder*—First, attach a wire or string to the top of the pinecone and make a hanging loop (see illustration). Use a finger or a spoon to cover the pinecone with peanut butter. When the whole cone is covered, roll it in birdseed. Hang the feeder from a tree branch.

• *Fruit Feeder*—Cut a very ripe orange or grapefruit in half. Use both halves as feeders. Find two broken tree branches that will poke through the fruit halves (see illustration). Place one half on each branch. This should be replaced or removed after two days.

• *Popcorn Feeder*—Thread a needle with a thread about two feet long. String popcorn on the thread and tie the ends together to make a popcorn necklace. Hang it over a branch (see illustration).

Once the feeders are made and placed in trees, players may start watching for birds to come. Players should keep track of how many birds and how many different kinds of birds they see coming to each feeder they are watching. Use a bird book to identify different birds. The one who sees the most birds is the winner.

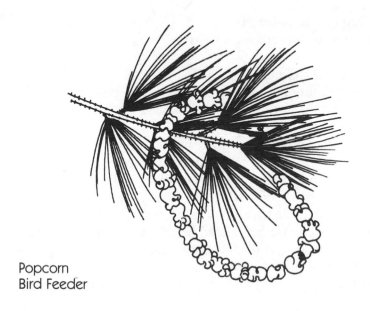

Popcorn
Bird Feeder

Different Ages, Different Stages:
Very young children can get in on the bird-feeding fun without having to make anything. Birds will flock to a place where bread crumbs are being sprinkled around. Hand over a bag of crumbs to the youngest siblings and let them do their own thing.

Older children who are good with a hammer and nails may think it's fun to build a more elaborate bird feeder. Check the local library for craft books with detailed instructions on building birdhouses and feeders.

Then Try This!
Keep a camera handy and be prepared to take photographs of nature's feathered visitors. When the pictures are developed, make a bird scrapbook.

◆ Nature Hunt ◆
(ALL AGES)

1 or more players

Materials:
paper bag for each player
list of things to collect for each player

Object of the Game:
To go on a nature hunt in search of specific items on a list.

How to Play:
Nature is full of interesting and beautiful things. Whether your surroundings are in the city, suburbs, or country, there are many things to be found. Parents or older siblings may make up the list of objects for which to look. A sample list might include: a leaf, a blade of grass, a pinecone, a quartz rock, a dandelion, a bird's feather, a seed pod, an acorn, a piece of tree bark not on the tree, and a flat stone. Make the list appropriate to the area in which you live.

Give a copy of the list and a paper bag for collecting to each player. Set a time limit appropriate to the number of items on the list—half an hour for ten items. Players should scour the hunt area until they find all the items on the list. The first one to find them all is the winner.

Different Ages, Different Stages:
A child may play this game alone or with others. The fun is in the finding. Younger siblings who can't read the list can still be included in the hunting fun. Send the younger ones on a hunt for one thing at a time while the older siblings search with the list in hand.

Then Try This!
Turn this Nature Hunt into a Save Nature Hunt. Instead of listing items of nature, make up a list of items that might hurt nature. The list might include: a bottle cap, a plastic bag, a candy wrapper, a piece of wire, a soda can, a juice box, a plastic milk bottle cap ring, and a drinking straw. The first one to find all the items on the list is the winner.

◆ Out to Lunch ◆
(AGES 3 AND UP)

2 or more players

Materials:
paper and pencil
bag lunch for each player
picnic blanket

Object of the Game:
To follow written clues that lead to a hidden treasure—lunch—then have an outdoor picnic.

How to Play:
Combine the fun of hiking, exploring, treasure hunting, and eating a picnic lunch. Set out the fixings for a perfect picnic

61

lunch—sandwich fixings, fruit, carrot sticks, cookies, chips, and drinks. Let the players prepare their own bag lunches.

While the players are preparing their bag lunches, an older sibling or parent may prepare the clues that will be placed around the yard and the hiking path, and will finally lead the players to lunch. Here are some examples of the kinds of clues to use.

- *Clue #1—Walk ten steps to the right*
  And if you do
  You will find
  Clue #2

- *Clue #2—Follow your nose*
  And you will see
  Where the flowers are
  Is Clue #3.

- *Clue #3—Run 'round the house*
  Two times or more
  Stop at the pine tree
  There's Clue #4!

and so on until the last clue, which might be something like this:

- *Clue #10—Nine clues found—*
  That's quite a bunch!
  This last clue leads
  you straight to lunch.
  Walk down the path
  About twenty feet,
  That's where you'll find
  Something to eat!

When the players have finished preparing their lunches, an adult or older child should take the bags to a chosen eating spot to which the clues finally lead the players. Spread a picnic blanket on the ground at the picnic spot and have it all ready for the players when they find it.

Different Ages, Different Stages:
The ages of the players will determine the difficulty of the clues and the length of the hiking course. Younger players can just follow arrow clues around their own yard. Older players can really be led on a good, long hike that may only end up back in the yard. A picnic doesn't always have to be a lunch. Out to Snack works just as well.

Then Try This!
Add to the hunting fun by hiding juice boxes, well-wrapped desserts, and peanuts in their shells around the yard and under bushes. Let everyone do the hunting and then divide up the goodies evenly.

◆ Sounds of Nature ◆
(AGES 4 AND UP)

2 or more players

Materials:
cassette tape player
blank tape

Object of the Game:
To record sounds of nature and identify them correctly later.

How to Play:
A tape recorder is easy to operate and opens the world of sound and good listening skills to children of all ages. The sounds of nature can be missed unless ears are trained to hear them, so this game is fun and educational.

One player or team of players begins by inserting a blank tape into a tape recorder. They then go outside and start re-

63

cording and taking notes. As they walk around to different areas of the yard, block, or place where they usually play, the tape recorder will pick up the sounds of birds chirping, crickets singing, leaves rustling, and wind blowing. It will also pick up other sounds such as dogs barking, cars going by, airplanes flying overhead, sanitation people banging the garbage cans, and so on. When one or both sides of the tape are filled, it may be rewound and listened to in a quiet place. How many sounds of nature can the other player or players correctly identify? The player with the most correct sound identifications is the winner.

Different Ages, Different Stages:
Older siblings can record very specific sounds, such as a toilet flushing, a parent sneezing, and a refrigerator door closing. They then may challenge parents or friends to identify the sounds. Younger children may listen to a Sounds of Nature tape and be asked to tell which sounds are sounds of nature and which sounds were made by other things. For example: birds' songs are nature sounds, airplane engines are other sounds.

Then Try This!
In addition to recording the sounds of nature, siblings should be encouraged to talk to each other about how it makes them feel when they look up at the sky or feel the breeze blow on their faces. Playing back the recording of these conversations will be a special treat, especially at a later date.

OFF TO THE RACES

On your mark, get set, go! Whether these games involve walking, running, rolling, or throwing, the object is to be the first to reach a goal. Speed is not the main thing here. Accuracy and coordination are the keys to success at these races.

◆ Paper Chase ◆

2 or more players

Materials:
2 sheets of newspaper per player

Object of the Game:
To be the first to reach the finish line.

How to Play:
The race is on and the winner is the player who reaches the finish line first. Mark a starting place and a finish line. Give each player two sheets from a newspaper. On the word "Go" players put one newspaper sheet down on the ground in front of them and step on it. Next, they put the other piece of newspaper down and step onto it, pick up the first piece and place it down in front again. The point is to create a newspaper path, one sheet at a time, all the way to the finish line. Players must reach the line by stepping from sheet to sheet.

Different Ages, Different Stages:
This may be more difficult for younger players who have trouble balancing as they turn around and bend down to pick up the sheet behind them. Give these players the advantage of a shorter course and two pieces of 8½" × 11" construction paper rather than newspaper sheets. Instead of moving the finish line closer, move the starting place closer only for the youngest players.

Then Try This!
Make a newspaper ball with each sheet. Mark a target on a tree or fence. Take aim with the paper balls and practice hitting the target.

Argument Ender #6

"He's not following the rules!"

After it is established that the offender truly is following his own drummer, assure the other player that this is indeed annoying. Then restate the rules. If the rebellious player balks at your instructions, suggest two options. Either the players stop playing or they discuss new rules that are mutually agreeable. This latter suggestion will give both players pause, and will often result in a creative new way to have fun.

◆

◆ Toe-to-Toe Roll ◆

(AGES 2 AND UP)

2 or more players

Materials:
none needed

Object of the Game:
For two players to roll across the ground or floor while keeping their toes touching each other's toes.

How to Play:
This is the easiest fun to have because all that is needed are two players and their toes. Find a soft, grassy area in which to roll. Check the area for sticks and any other debris and remove it.

Both players lie on the ground with their legs out straight and their feet touching each other's feet. They do not hold hands, they only touch toes and feet. When their feet are lined up, the two players must try to roll across the ground together while keeping their toes touching. With two players, it's good for an outdoor giggle. With four players or more, this can be a great rolling race.

Different Ages, Different Stages:
Younger children actually have an easier time with this game because their legs are shorter and easier to control. However, if it seems too difficult for some players to really keep their toes touching, just let the rolling part be the fun. Racing down a small hill in a rolling position with arms stretched out straight over the head brings squeals of delight from all children.

Then Try This!
Turn the Toe-to-Toe Roll into a triathlon. Have the rolling be Part I. Choose a goal to run to as Part II. Hop back to the starting point as Part III.

◆ Plate Sailing ◆
(AGES 4 AND UP)

2 or more players

Materials:
cardboard box
5 paper plates

Object of the Game:
To toss paper plates into a targeted box.

How to Play:
Sailing paper plates through the air is as much fun as skipping stones across a lake. The trick to doing it well is all in the wrist. Before playing the game, players should practice holding a paper plate between their thumb and next two fingers. Curve the plate in toward the wrist, then turn it out sideways like a Frisbee and throw it. Once players have gotten the wrist action under control, the game can begin.

Set a box down and stand back about ten or fifteen feet from where players will stand. Players take turns trying to sail five plates into the box. Each plate that goes in counts as one point. The first player to gain ten points wins the game or the round. Players may decide how many points to play per game.

Different Ages, Different Stages:
The youngest plate sailers may feel more comfortable standing six to eight feet away from the box. For them, throwing the plate is just as acceptable as sailing it. Very young ones who don't want to be in a contest will have fun being the official "plate boy" or "plate girl." Give them the job of gathering the tossed plates and bringing them back to the players.

Then Try This!
Turn the time into an arts and crafts time too. Let the players use markers to decorate their plates and create extra-special flyers for the game.

◆ Duck Walk ◆
(AGES 6 AND UP)

2 or more players

Materials:
none needed

Object of the Game:
To be the first to cross the finish line.

How to Play:
Pretending to be anything other than human can be fun. Pretending to be a duck is not only fun but also hysterically embarrassing. Here's how the game is played.

Mark a finish line ten to fifteen feet from the start. On the word "Go!" players bend down in a stooped position. They grasp their ankles with their hands and begin trying to walk to the finish line. The one who crosses the finish line first is the winner.

Different Ages, Different Stages:
Younger siblings may not be able to stay balanced and walk in the stooped position. Allow them to hold their knees instead of their ankles. Adjust the starting line for them so that it is closer to the finish line. Or let the younger players start a few seconds sooner. The race can be made more difficult for the older players by having them race to the finish line, turn around, and race back to the start.

Then Try This!
Duck Walk is a perfect relay race for teams of racers. Try it at the next party and see. Divide the group into two teams. The first two racers go to the finish line, come back to the start, and tag the next racers. The first entire team to complete the races wins.

Argument Ender #7

"You didn't jump in time! That doesn't count!"

In games where a time limit is given, avoid overtime arguments by using a simple kitchen timer. Reset the timer for each player and each turn. If someone jumps in, or starts running, or finishes running after the timer has signaled the time has run out, he or she must let the timer be the judge.

◆

HAVE A BALL

Take a ball outdoors and the sky is the limit! Balls of all sizes provide all kinds of fun. Ping-Pong, tennis, basketball, baseball, volleyball, football, kickball, soccer—they're all a ball to play.

And the balls designed for specific games can certainly be used in other games too. But no ball is so versatile as an ordinary playground ball, and this trio of ball games puts a new spin on it.

◆ High Bounce ◆

(AGES 4 AND UP)

2 or more players

Materials:
playground ball
cardboard box or small trash can

Object of the Game:
To bounce the ball into the container from varying distances.

How to Play:
Trying to get a ball into a container in one bounce is a challenge for a player of any age. It sounds like an easy thing to do, but in fact it's not. Place the box or can in one spot. Players must stand back three feet from the "basket" and aim with the ball. On the next turn, players stand back five feet and try again to bounce the ball once into the "basket." Players move back an additional two feet for each turn, always trying to get the ball in on one bounce. Stop at ten or twelve feet and start over again. One point is scored for each try. If it takes three tries to get the ball in, three points are scored. The player with the lowest point score is the winner.

Different Ages, Different Stages:
Younger players who are not ready to aim and bounce a ball might do better rolling the ball into a container tipped onto its side. Older players can add more challenge to the game by also having a contest for the highest bounce on each turn.

Then Try This!
While the ball is out and being bounced, stage other ball-bouncing contests. Who can bounce the ball the longest? The highest? The lowest? Under a leg the most times? Against a wall the most times?

◆ Backward Bowling ◆

(AGES 4 AND UP)

2 or more players

Materials:
playground ball or soccer ball
10 empty milk cartons or plastic soda bottles

Object of the Game:
To throw the ball backward, between the legs, and knock down as many "pins" as possible.

How to Play:
No heavy bowling balls, no clunky shoes to rent, and no head-aches from the noise of the tenpins falling down.

On a driveway or smooth playground area, set up the bowling "pins" in a triangle just like real pins are set up in a bowling alley. Mark a starting line about ten feet from the pins. Players take turns rolling the ball twice on each turn—just like real bowling. However, in this game players stand facing away from the pins. With feet apart, they bend over, look through their legs, and try to roll the ball straight at the pins. Play ten frames and keep score by adding up the number of pins knocked down by each player in each frame. There are no strikes or spares. If all the pins are knocked down on the first roll, the next player goes. The player with the highest score is the winner.

Different Ages, Different Stages:
Give the younger players a break. Let them face the pins and bowl the right way. It's easier and will allow even very young

71

ones to get in on the bowling fun. Appoint one young sibling to be in charge of setting up the pins between frames.

Then Try This!
Bowling on a smaller scale can be big fun. Instead of a ball and milk cartons or soda bottles, use a marble and clothespins or a smaller ball such as a tennis ball or Ping-Pong ball and empty plastic spice bottles.

Argument Ender #8

"She laughed!"

Stop the accusations and keep the game going with a few sentences that tell each arguer you understand and are listening: "Games can be funny. As long as you're laughing at how silly this all is, and not making fun of each other, then laughing is fine. Otherwise you're being mean, and that's not allowed." The accuser will know you paid attention to his or her feelings. The accused will be excused just this once if guilty, and be glad of it.

◆

CHALK IT UP

A little chalk goes a long way, but a lot of chalk goes even farther. Driveways, sidewalks, and paved playground surfaces are the perfect places for chunky sidewalk chalk fun and games. It's easy for all ages to apply, and nature does the cleaning up. What could be better?

◆ Hopscotch ◆

2 players or more

Materials:
chalk
marker for each player (bottle cap, stone, or some other flat object)
pavement

Object of the Game:
To hop through a chalk-drawn game board without touching the lines or losing balance.

How to Play:
Even though memories of Hopscotch may include girls only, it's a sidewalk game that's fun and challenging for boys too. This classic chalk game can be played anywhere there is pavement on which to draw the game board. There are many different possibilities for game boards. Here is just one of them.

Using a piece of sidewalk chalk, draw a game board like the one shown on the next page. Make each section about twelve inches square so that it is large enough to accommodate a player's foot but small enough so that the lines present a slight risk. Where there is one square, players will hop into it on one foot. Where there are two squares side by side, players will straddle the middle line and keep a foot in each square.

Each player has a marker that can be easily identified as his or her own. The first player should stand outside the line of the game board and toss the marker into the first space. The marker must not touch any of the lines on the box. The player then hops on one foot into space 1 and bends down to pick up the marker while still standing on one foot. The player then turns around, still on one foot, and returns to the outside of the game board. The next player takes a turn on space 1. When all players have completed the first space, the first player then

73

throws the marker into space 2. The player then hops on one foot to space 1 and jumps onto spaces 2 and 3, straddling the middle line with one foot in 2 and one foot in 3. The marker is picked up and the player turns around and hops back. Players take turns until all players have gotten all the way through the game board. If a player steps on a line he or she must start over again. The first player to successfully get through all the spaces without touching a line is the winner.

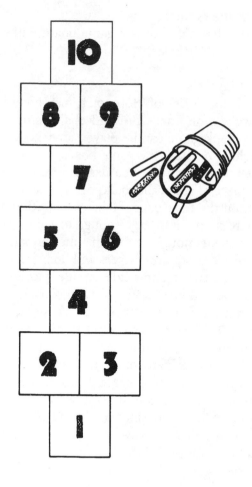

Hopscotch
Game Board

Different Ages, Different Stages:

Hopscotch can be as difficult or as easy as players want it to be. Younger players can draw a simplified board with all double boxes so no one-foot hopping is required. Older players can make the game board longer than ten spaces so throwing the marker accurately becomes more difficult. Siblings can play side-by-side on two separate game boards, or rules can be relaxed for the younger players.

Then Try This!

Here's another version of the game board that adds extra fun to the game of Hopscotch. This game calls for all one-foot hopping, and because it is shaped like a snail (see illustration), it is more difficult to navigate without losing balance. The rules of play are the same.

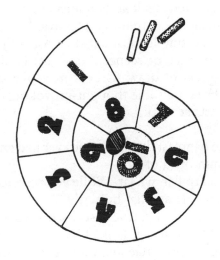

Hopscotch
Game Board

◆ Sidewalk Art Show ◆

1 or more players

Materials:
chalk (the more colors the better)
pavement

Object of the Game:
To create an outdoor art show of chalk artwork for all to see.

How to Play:
There are no rules. There is no right or wrong. Chalk art is an activity that encourages freedom of artistic expression. The play is art; the players are the artists.

Each artist is given chalk and an area of driveway, sidewalk, or other pavement free of traffic as a "canvas" on which to work. Drawings may be simple, abstract designs, realistic likenesses of animals or objects, or scenes. Some artists like to think of their own subjects to draw. Others may like suggestions or assignments. Here are some thought-provoking ideas that may inspire the artists at work:

- Think of the happiest dream you've ever had and draw something to remind you of it.
- You had a caterpillar in a jar. While you were asleep it turned into a butterfly. Draw that butterfly.
- You're a scientist and you've just discovered another planet. Draw a picture of what it looks like.
- There's a big, empty circle just waiting for a face to be drawn in it. You draw the face you'd like to see.
- While exploring your grandmother's attic you found an old trunk. You opened it up and were amazed to see . . . What? Draw a picture of something in that trunk.
- Some people say there's a pot of gold at the end of a rainbow. Draw a picture of something you think could be at the end of the rainbow.

Different Ages, Different Stages:
When the canvas is as big as all outdoors, younger artists may get bored or discouraged before they complete a picture. Let an older sibling define a drawing area for a younger one. A simple chalk outline the size of a piece of paper can make the activity seem more manageable. Also the older child might draw a small portion of a picture for the younger one to complete—for instance, the rainbow. Older artists should be encouraged to spread out and enjoy the freedom offered by large spaces.

Then Try This!
Take a picture, it lasts longer. Chalk art only lasts as long as the fair weather does. Take photographs of the artists at work and their masterpieces when they are finished.

◆ Chalk Trails ◆

2 or more players

Materials:
chalk (a different color for each player)
1 treasure for each player (secret note, special snack treat, etc.)

Object of the Game:
To be the first to find the treasure at the end of a chalk trail.

How to Play:
Chalk trails are fun to make whether they lead to treasures or not. It is a treat for children to take a walk and leave a trail of chalk marks along the way just so they can find their way home again. But a spiral trail that leads to a surprise treasure adds an extra element of excitement to the activity.

Each player chooses a different color of chalk and is given

a "treasure" to hide. Each player will create a chalk trail for another player to follow. Beginning at the same starting point, players start making a chalk trail leading away from the others. The trails should be more than just straight lines. Loops and mazelike circles that crisscross each other and lead followers in circles make the trails more interesting. Design the trail so that it goes from the starting point, down the driveway, around the block, or wherever players are able to go safely. At the end of their trails, each player should leave a small treasure such as a note saying "Congratulations! You made it!" or an apple or other snack treat. Every trail leads to some surprise. After the trails are drawn, players meet back at the start and switch trails so they are following another player's trail instead of their own. Players must walk along the chalk trail, following it exactly as it is drawn. Everyone's a winner when the treasure is reached.

Different Ages, Different Stages:
Younger players may get confused by lots of different-colored marks. They will enjoy making a simple trail with construction paper arrows or some mark of their own leading simply from one spot on a driveway or sidewalk to another.

Older players can make their chalk trails long and complicated, taking their opponents on a good long hike through the neighborhood. There's no worry about anyone getting lost. The chalk trail will lead them home again.

Then Try This!
When children are first given the privilege and responsibility of walking to a friend's house in the neighborhood, give them pieces of chalk to take along. As they walk, they can make their marks all along the way. Seeing the chalk marks when it's time to walk home again is reassuring and fun.

Argument Ender #9

"I don't want to play anymore!"

Sometimes one sibling will tire of a game way before another, which can frustrate the avid player tremendously. First try suggesting that the reluctant player give the game a few more minutes, thus giving the other sibling a chance to wind down while still enjoying the game. In this way he or she won't feel so abruptly cut off from pleasure. If this doesn't work, simply suggest to the sibling who doesn't want to play that he or she go off and entertain himself or herself, and then, if possible, wind down the game with the other player yourself, saying, "I'll do it with you for a minute or two and then we'll be done."

The bottom line is you can't insist children play. The spirit has to be there. Otherwise it's just a bad one-act play.

◆

◆ Chapter 5 ◆

Hot and Bothered

Fun for Sticky, Buggy, Battle-Prone Days

WHEN THE SUN is beating down, beating boredom is the hot topic. Finding some cool things to do on the hottest days is easy. Just breeze through the activities in this chapter and you'll welcome the heat-beating selection of things to do when the kids feel burned out.

MADE IN THE SHADE

Make the shade a shade more interesting with this batch of lazy-day activities made to be played in the shade. Spread a big old blanket out under a big old shade tree and start having a big old bunch of fun.

◆ Hat Crafts ◆

1 or more players

Materials:
plain white painter's hat for each player
colored fabric markers
fabric glue
decorative craft items (buttons, sequins, feathers, etc.)

Object of the Project:
To create a hat that will block out the hot sun and look very cool at the same time.

How to Play:
On a hot day a cool thing to do is sit in the shade and make a hat to wear when you're out in the sun.

Provide each hatmaker with a plain white painter's hat and a box full of fabric markers, glue, and decorative items. Let each player know that anything goes. Use the markers to create designs or to write slogans on the hats. Dress them up by gluing on sequins, buttons, feathers, or anything else that changes a plain hat into a designer original.

Different Ages, Different Stages:
If the age difference between siblings is great, divide the materials evenly among them rather than putting them all in one big box. Avoid arguments over who has the best stuff by making sure each artist has the same materials. Older siblings can help the younger ones apply glue in small amounts and can also help with writing names or words on their hats. Both older and younger siblings can work together on a hat for the very youngest sibling who may not be old enough to make a hat but would love to wear one.

81

Then Try This!

Let handmade hats be the showstopper costumes in a sunny-day play. Select a play or skit from a book in the library, or let the players make up their own play. Have the players make a hat for each character and then wear the hats as they act out their parts in the play.

Argument Ender #10

"He's taking all the best stuff!"

Stop this argument before it starts. When siblings are working together on craft projects that include craft materials, make sure each child has his or her own materials box. Before play begins, check to see that both boxes have exactly the same materials available.

◆ Watermelon Fun ◆

(AGES 4 AND UP)

2 or more players

Materials:
watermelon

Object of the Game:
To spit watermelon seeds the farthest distance.

How to Play:
On a hot day ice-cold watermelon hits the spot. Turn the cool feast into a fun feast with a good old-fashioned watermelon seed-spitting contest.

Give each player a piece of watermelon to eat. As they eat

and come across a seed, players should get ready, take aim, and fire the seed out as far as they can spit it. The player who sends a seed the longest distance wins the round and scores one point. Keep track of points. The player with the most points wins.

Different Ages, Different Stages:
Even little watermelon lovers can be in the contest as long as they are old enough to hold a seed in their mouths without choking on it. Move the starting line up for little spitters. Make the game more difficult for the older ones by having a target or a cup at which they must aim.

Then Try This!
Surprise everyone at the next picnic with this colorful watermelon trick. You'll need a whole watermelon and one quart of real grape juice (see illustration). To do this successfully, the watermelon must be cold. Place it in the refrigerator for a few hours before starting. Cut three one-inch squares out of the

Purple Watermelon Trick

melon rind (one at each end and one in the middle) and save them. Be sure to cut all the way through to the melon. Slowly pour the grape juice into each hole, one hole at a time. After pouring in about half the juice, put the rind squares back in place and return the melon to the refrigerator. After an hour, take it out and pour in the rest of the juice. When the watermelon is sliced, picnicgoers will be tickled purple when they see the world's one and only purple watermelon!

◆ Dandy Dandelion Chains ◆

(AGES 6 AND UP)

1 or more players

Materials:
yard full of dandelions

Object of the Project:
To make a decorative chain out of dandelions.

How to Play:
Dandelions are those little yellow flowers that come up on even the nicest lawns. They look too pretty to be weeds, but guess what? They are. So picking them is definitely allowed, and turning them into something else is an activity just made for a lazy, sunny day. Pick a basketful of dandelions, keeping the stems as long as possible. Then spread out a blanket under a good shade tree and start chaining.

Because of their very flexible stems, dandelions can be tied into chains and then tied at the ends and worn as bracelets, floral headbands, necklaces, or ankle bracelets. Begin the chain by tying the stems of two flowers together at the ends. Add the next flower by tying the stem around the underneath part of the dandelion. Keep adding on until your dandelion chain is as long as you want it to be. Make jewelry or have a contest to see who can make the longest chain. Adorn fences, doorways, or tree branches with the yellow dandelion chains. This old-fashioned activity never goes out of style.

Different Ages, Different Stages:
Let the younger siblings do the dandelion picking and the older ones do the chain making. Little ones will be glad to sit and watch if they know some of the chains being made will end up on their own wrists and around their necks.

Then Try This!
While children are outside looking for dandelions, suggest that they keep their eyes out for a lucky four-leaf clover as well. Sitting on a blanket spread next to a patch of clover is a great low-energy activity for a hot day.

◆ Story Hour ◆
(ALL AGES)

2 or more players

Materials:
blanket
cool drink for each player
imagination

Object of the Project:
To create and share stories outdoors in the shade.

How to Play:
Storytelling is one of the earliest forms of entertainment. Creating stories or just telling true tales is a cool thing to do on a hot day. After a day of active play, this is a good way to make use of a little quiet time.

Make the moment special by making it an event. Have a special Story Hour blanket that can be spread out on the ground in a cool, shady spot. Give each player a cool drink to sip as he or she rests comfortably on the blanket and joins in the fun of creating a story with someone else. Stories told may be true or made up. For creating stories, give the players some beginning sentences and let them complete the story with their own ideas. Here are some possible story starters.

- The wind howled and the tree branches knocked on the window. Inside, a little black dog named Pepper pressed his nose against the glass. He was looking for . . .
- When the children woke up and saw their mother standing in the kitchen wearing a clown costume, they knew this was going to be a very unusual day. "Get dressed, kids," said Mom the clown. "We're going to . . ."
- For almost a whole year, the house next door to ours had a For Sale sign in the front yard. This morning the sign was gone. I heard strange sounds coming from inside the house. Imagine my surprise when I peeked in the window and saw . . .

Different Ages, Different Stages:
Story Hour gives children of all ages the opportunity to put some of their experiences into words. It should be clear that the stories told may be based on real events and enhanced with made-up events. Younger siblings' stories may be simply a retelling of a dream they had, something funny that happened at the grocery store, or a report on something seen while riding in a car. Setting aside this special time will encourage communication between siblings and will help teach good listening skills as well.

Then Try This!
A tape recorder and blank cassettes make a great addition to the Story Hour. Older readers can read and record books on tape for younger siblings. The tapes can be played back on car trips or on rainy days when younger siblings are looking for something to do.

SPLISH SPLASH WATER FUN

On a hot and steamy day how do you spell relief? W-A-T-E-R! Believe it or not, some people don't live steps away from a nice cold ocean. For those who open the door and see no sea, the hose is the next best thing. Wash away the red-hot blues with these chilling ideas for playtime.

◆ Hose Tag ◆

(AGES 3 AND UP)

2 or more players

Materials:
garden hose with adjustable spray nozzle
water

Object of the Game:
To tag a player with a stream of water from the hose.

How to Play:
Running around in the heat sounds like a bad idea until you add a cool stream of water sprayed from a hose. This version of the classic game of Tag gives relief from the heat while allowing active players to let off steam.

Hook up a garden hose and give it to one player, who will be "It." Before the game begins, choose a spot that will be "Home Base," and decide on boundaries within which players must stay. The player who is "It" must try to catch the other players by getting them wet with the stream of water from the hose. The other players must run and try to avoid being tagged by the water. If a player touches Home Base he or she is safe from becoming "It" until leaving Home. When a player is tagged by the hose, that player becomes "It." The game goes on until the players have had enough and are ready to cool off in the spray of the hose just for the fun of it.

Different Ages, Different Stages:
Older children should be cautioned to adust the spray nozzle to a fine spray. Rules should be established as to which areas of the body should not be sprayed. The face, for instance, should be off-limits unless everyone playing agrees to allow it. Younger siblings won't be able to escape the hose as easily as the older ones, so give the little players the option of being tagged three times before they become "It."

Then Try This!
While the hose is out, make a rainbow. Stand with the sun shining from behind and spray the hose with a fine spray. The sunlight caught in the spray makes a beautiful rainbow. Little ones will like to run through it.

◆ Hose Limbo ◆
(AGES 3 AND UP)

2 or more players

Materials:
garden hose with adjustable spray nozzle
water

Object of the Game:
To duck under a stream of water without getting wet.

How to Play:
"How low can you go?" That's the whole idea in the game of Limbo. But in Hose Limbo, instead of ducking under a pole, game players duck under a stream of water.

With one person holding the hose as high up as possible, the spray nozzle should be adjusted to a strong and steady spray. The player holding the hose points the spray out straight. The other player or players must walk under the stream once, trying not to get wet. The stream is lowered a little more for each turn until the players ducking under it can't even crawl under without getting wet. The player who can go the lowest and stay dry is the winner.

Different Ages, Different Stages:
The taller players should be the hose holders. The game will best be played by players old enough to balance themselves as they lean backward to try to duck under the hose. Younger players will just enjoy ducking under and getting wet even if that technically means they lose. On a hot day, getting wet is a winning idea for all ages.

Then Try This!
Watch the birds play Hose Limbo too. Set up the hose in a tree limb and adjust the nozzle to a fine spray. The birds will fly through the shower and feel as refreshed as the children do.

◆ Sprinkler Jump ◆
(AGES 4 AND UP)

1 or more players

Materials:
garden hose
sprinkler that turns around
water

Object of the Game:
To jump over the stream of water each time it comes around.

How to Play:
When the beach is out of reach, go for the sprinkler instead. Set up a sprinkler that goes around in a circle. Players should wear bathing suits, because they will get wet no matter how good they are at jumping. Turn on the sprinkler and when the stream of water comes to a player, he or she must jump over it. Players should try to set a record for the number of successful jumps, then try to beat that record.

Different Ages, Different Stages:
Little sprinkler jumpers will just enjoy running and dancing in and out of the sprinkler instead of trying not to get wet. Let them keep count of how many times they do get wet. The real point for all ages is to cool off with a safe water-play activity.

Then Try This!
Set up the sprinkler on a hot summer night. Even the oldest players in the house will think it's exciting and fun to run through the water in the dark. Everyone will feel more free to dance and play in the water when the moon is the only light.

Argument Ender #11

"She's being mean to me!"

Restate the rules of the home: There is no name-calling, no sarcasm, no comparing, and no negative comments allowed. When the game is resumed, if any of these rules are broken, the game must stop immediately. The one who has been mean must then be separated from the other player with instructions to think about what she or he might have done differently so that the game could have continued. The wronged player should enjoy some small privilege as a consolation. After approximately ten minutes, if the player given the time-out is ready to admit his or her mistake and get on with the game, let the playing commence once again!

◆

◆ Body Painting ◆

(AGES 4 AND UP)

1 or more players

Materials:
garden hose
paintbrushes
watercolor paints
bucket of water

Object of the Project:
To cool off creatively by painting designs on the body and then washing them off with the hose.

How to Play:
When it's hot enough to wear a bathing suit, body painting adds a colorful extra to hose or sprinkler play. Set out the paints and brushes and fill a bucket with water for brush dipping. Players may work alone or together to paint their own or each other's bodies. Designs can be anything—from stripes and polka dot patterns, to solid-colored arms and legs, to fancier tattoolike designs painted here, there, and everywhere. Anything goes, and when it's finished it all disappears with a little help from the garden hose. Wash away the artwork and cool off at the same time. This activity raises hose play to a fine art activity.

Different Ages, Different Stages:
Younger players may not want their designs washed off right away. Keep a mirror handy so they can see their work. Older players can try their hands at face painting on the younger siblings. Everyone can get in on the hosing down when the painting is done.

Then Try This!

Every picture tells a story. Be sure to photograph the artists at work and the finished painted bodies, so the story of the body painting day will be remembered by all.

◆ Hose Statues ◆

(AGES 4 AND UP)

4 or more players

Materials:
garden hose with adustable spray nozzle
water

Object of the Game:
To reach the finish line without getting caught and sprayed with water by the caller.

How to Play:
This version of the classic game Moving Statues has been adapted for play on those hot days when the only relief in sight is the garden hose. Bathing suits should be worn, because players will get wet.

Mark both a starting line and a finish line about thirty to fifty feet apart, depending on the space available. Choose one player to be the caller. The caller stands at the finish line holding a hose. The other players line up along the starting line.

The game begins when the caller turns and faces away from the players. He or she counts to ten out loud while the players move forward toward the finish line as fast as they can. However, players must be ready to stop immediately and stand motionless as soon as the caller turns around and faces them. Anyone caught moving gets sprayed with the hose and must return to the starting line. The first player to reach the finish line becomes the next caller.

Different Ages, Different Stages:

Younger players may not be as good at stopping and standing perfectly still. Adjust the rules to allow them to choose between being sprayed or returning to the starting line. Older players may be able to run too fast and get too far on the count of ten. To make the game more challenging for them, have the caller count only to five.

Then Try This!

Add a little more mystery to the game by adding a blindfold to the caller. The caller stands in the middle and the other players stand anywhere they like within thirty feet of the caller. The caller calls out "Wet!" The players call out "Dry!" from wherever they are and then run to another spot. The caller must try to figure out where a player might be and spray him or her with the hose. The first player sprayed is the next caller.

◆ Swing! ◆

(AGES 3 AND UP)

1 or more players

Materials:

swing
garden hose
fan sprinkler

Object of the Game:

To swing and race against the spray of the sprinkler.

How to Play:

On a breezeless day swinging on a swing creates its own breath of breeze. Adding a refreshing spray of water from the sprinkler adds a trickle of tickley good feelings to the swinging fun. Simply set up the fan sprinkler close enough to the swing so that when the swinger swings forward he or she will swing into the spray. A challenge may be added to the game by keeping the sprinkler's spray just far enough away so that it only touches the swinger who pumps hard and gets the swing far enough out to reach the spray. Players may race against the fan of spray and see how many times they can swing back and forth before the spray returns to meet them.

Different Ages, Different Stages:
Older children can push younger siblings who are not old enough to pump for themselves. While older children are swinging into the sprinkler spray, younger ones can stand back and run through the spray as it goes away from the swing. Older children should be cautioned not to jump off the swing and into the water. The grass could be dangerously slippery—and younger siblings may try to imitate the actions of the older players.

Then Try This!
Swinging is full of opportunities for contests. Who can swing the highest? Who can twist the swing around and let it unwind the fastest? Who can pump for the longest time? Who can swing into the water the most times? Take the swing contest challenges and then cool off in the sprinkler.

WATER WORKS

Working with water makes working on a hot day more play than work. Here are some "jobs" that combine the pleasures of work and play—and cool off the workers while they're at it.

◆ Car Wash ◆
(AGES 4 AND UP)

1 or more players

Materials:
bucket of soapy water
sponge for each player

94

drying towels
garden hose

Object of the Project:
To wash a car and cool off.

How to Play:
Washing the family car has a valuable outcome even if there's no income from it. Whether it's done for money or just for fun, siblings working together on this will love the opportunity to do some work that feels like play.

Provide a bucket full of soapy water and a sponge for each car washer. Turn the garden hose on low and instruct the workers to spray the car first just to wash off loose dirt. Then they can divide the car into sections and each take one. Make a contest to see who finishes a section first. At the word "Go!" players begin soaping the car and getting the deeper dirt off. When the whole section of the car has been scrubbed, turn the hose on again and rinse away the soapy water. Drying towels should be used to wipe away the drips. Depending on the age and ability of each player, more professional car-cleaning products can be used, but even soap and water bring a shine to the car and a smile to the faces of the washers. The first to finish a section gets a time-out to get wet with the hose, or gets to spray the other washers.

Different Ages, Different Stages:
There is something for everyone to do in car washing. Little ones can be assigned to the lower portions of the car. Giving them the responsibility of cleaning the bumpers or hubcaps offers a manageable duty and the opportunity for a real feeling of accomplishment. Older children will appreciate a parent's appreciation expressed in the form of payment. Money, of course, is not the only way to compensate for a job well done. A trip to the ice cream parlor or just a Popsicle from the home freezer can be enough of a reward.

Then Try This!

Older car washers really can make some spending money if they are serious about washing other people's cars. Signs advertising the place, time, and cost can be placed around the neighborhood. Working with a friend makes it a fun money-making event.

◆ Bike Wash ◆

(AGES 3 AND UP)

1 or more players

Materials:
bucket of soapy water
sponge for each player
drying towels
garden hose

Object of the Project:
To wash bikes and cool off.

How to Play:
Taking pride in keeping one's bicycle clean is a good thing for children of all ages to learn. Because bicycles are children's main means of transportation, they should enjoy keeping them clean and sparkling.

As with a car wash, provide a bucket full of soapy water and a sponge for each bike washer. Turn the garden hose on low and instruct the workers to spray the bike first just to wash off loose dirt. *Keep water off hand gears and hand brakes.* Use the sponge to soap up the bike, then rinse away the soapy water with clean water from a garden hose turned on low. When the bike is washed, dry it thoroughly with the drying towels.

Different Ages, Different Stages:
Bikes, Big Wheels, wagons, or wheeled pull toys—it makes no difference what's being washed. Older children will do a more

thorough job of cleaning their bikes, but even the youngest siblings can get in on the fun by washing their own set of wheels. If an older child decides to wash a bike, give the younger sibling something, anything, else to work on. This is a good side-by-side job rather than an all-in-it-together task.

Then Try This!
Turn the day into Bike Beautification Day. Add streamers to handlebars and playing cards to spokes to make that *clickety-clack* noise when the wheels go around, tighten screws, add mirrors, and fix or polish anything else to make the bike more beautiful.

◆ Stuffed Animal Wash ◆
(AGES 3 AND UP)

2 or more players

Materials:
washable stuffed animals and/or dolls
gentle detergent
washcloth
soft scrub brush
large washtub
garden hose

Object of the Project:
To wash stuffed animals and/or dolls and to cool off.

How to Play:
While older siblings are washing cars or bikes, younger siblings can join in the hose fun and have a Stuffed Animal Wash. Players can wear bathing suits and enjoy spraying themselves as they rinse off the washed stuffed animals.

Wash only stuffed animals that are washable and won't be damaged by water in the eyes or water in the stuffing. Fill the washtub with water from the garden hose. Add enough detergent to make suds. Players should gently dip their stuffed animals into the soapy water and give them a bath using the washcloth and scrub brush to clean soiled areas. Squeeze out the water and dip again and again until the fur looks clean. When all the animals have been washed, lay them on the grass and rinse with the garden hose. An older sibling can help squeeze out the soap. Lay the animals outside to dry in the open air. While the stuffed animals are drying, their owners can turn the hose on themselves. One can hold the hose for the other while each has a turn taking a hose shower.

Different Ages, Different Stages:
Even the baby's playthings need freshening up. Let big brother or big sister do the toy washing for the youngest sibling. The baby may not recognize the favor, but the sibling doing the washing will have fun showing the newly washed stuffed animal to baby and taking all the credit for a job well done.

Then Try This!
Let the little ones use the soapy water left in the washtub to wash out the rags used on the car and bike by the older siblings. Rinse the rags with the hose and let everyone work together to hang them up to dry.

◆ Chapter 6 ◆

Freezed Out

Icy Games to Keep Away the Chill

WHEN THE WEATHER reports ice, snow, and freezing temperatures, don't panic over what to do with housebound children. Snow and ice are two of nature's best playtime gifts if the instructions for play come with it. Here are all the instructions you need to turn those cold and frosty days into heartwarming, fun-filled days as well.

NO BUSINESS LIKE SNOW BUSINESS

It's snowing! And that just might mean that children will be home from school and losing their cool because their friends across town are snowed in and can't come over to play. That's when siblings come in handy. Here are some cool snow-day classics that are sure to make snowbound siblings agree that there's no day like a snow day for some fun-filled family play.

◆ Snow Angels ◆

1 or more players

Materials:
snow

Object of the Game:
To lie down in the snow and make angels.

How to Play:
Making snow angels is just one of those snow things that every child should know about. It's as much a part of childhood as teething, but completely painless.

Players should be dressed in snow clothes. To make a snow-angel shape, the players must lie down flat on their backs with arms down at their sides and legs closed. They begin making the snow angel by moving both arms and both legs out to the side in the snow and bringing them back close to the body. The motion should be repeated as many times as necessary to make the shape of an angel. Players should carefully get up, trying not to step in their own angels. Once the players have seen their angel impressions, they can add decorations to the shapes to make artistic snow angels. Angels, like snowmen, can be beautified by adding stones for eyes, noses, and mouths. Use sticks to draw details on the angel gowns. Make a whole choir of angels across a play yard or school playground.

Different Ages, Different Stages:
All ages can make angels. Little angels may need a helping hand when it comes time to stand up. Older angels can show younger siblings how to make the right shape and help them decorate their own angel.

Then Try This!

Have children lie side by side with hands touching as they are spread out. When one set of angels is made, players can get up and lie down next to the finished ones and make more. Soon a chain of angels will reach across the snowy area.

♦ Snow Fort, Snow Fight ♦

(AGES 3 AND UP)

2 or more players

Materials:
buckets or other snow molds and forms
snow

Object of the Game:
To make two snow forts and then defend them in a snowball fight that aims at snowball targets.

How to Play:
Snow forts can be as simple or as elaborate as the snow architects like. Half the fun is in the design and building of the fort, the other half is in defending it.

Two players, or two teams of players, should choose fort locations that are opposite one another. To ensure that the forts will remain standing as long as possible, players should try to build where the sun won't melt their forts too soon, and away from driveways or walkways that others may want cleared of snow.

A fort can be just a wall made of giant snowballs lined up or placed in a circle. Or it can be made of bucket-shaped bricks of snow stacked one on top of another to make a wall high enough to duck down behind. Dress up the walls by making turret shapes or other castlelike shapes. Players should place snowballs every six inches or so on top of the walls. These will be the targets the other players will aim for when the snow fight begins. Each fort should have the same number of targets.

101

Players prepare for the snow fight by making equal piles of snowballs to be stored inside each snow fort and to be thrown at the snowball targets when the fight begins. When both players or teams have completed their forts and made their snowballs, the snow fight begins. Players aim at the target snowballs on their opponent's fort's walls. The first player to knock off all the target snowballs wins the fight.

Different Ages, Different Stages:
Younger siblings will want to be included in the snowball fight, but won't want to be caught in the crossfire of snowballs. Let the little ones have the job of piling up snowballs for throwing and smoothing out the inside walls of the fort.

Then Try This!
Steaming cups of hot chocolate make great snow fort or snow house treats. Call it "Fortification for the Troops." Bring some out to the snow builders and let them enjoy the contrast between cold snow and hot cocoa.

◆ Snow Art ◆
(AGES 3 AND UP)

1 or more players

Materials:
snow molds (plastic containers, cookie cutters, sand toys, etc.)
food coloring
snow

Object of the Project:
To make snow sculptures and colored snow designs.

How to Play:

Inside every snowstorm there's a snow sculpture trying to get out. Give the snow a hand and turn a pile of it into a form of art.

Players may use their hands and snow molds to create snow people, snow animals, and any snow objects. If given the instruction "Go out and make a snowman," most children will go out and make a snowman. But if they are encouraged to try new and different snow sculptures, players will use their imaginations as well as their hands.

Once the sculptures have been made, fill some paper cups halfway with water. Add a few drops of food coloring to each cup, one color per cup. Let the snow artists experiment by pouring small amounts of color on their sculptures to add features, clothing, and other decorations. Cups of coloring may also be used to color snowballs or to make pictures in the snow.

Different Ages, Different Stages:

Smaller children enjoy making smaller snow sculptures. Small snow creations don't tire the little ones out as quickly and they allow the players to experience the joy of finishing rather than the disappointment of quitting. Give the younger ones a tray on which to work, making it easier to carry their work inside to show parents. Older players who prefer to work alone on their own sculptures may encourage younger siblings to make smaller versions of the same sculpture.

Then Try This!

If snow shoveling isn't anyone's idea of a fun way to make money, selling snow sculptures might be. Older players can sell their sculpture services in the neighborhood. All they do is ring the doorbell of a friendly neighbor and ask if the neighbor would like to pay for a snow sculpture to be built in the front yard. Older neighbors who can't make their own snowman might enjoy seeing one in their yard. Do it for the fun of it or for a reasonable price. Try it!

Argument Ender #12

"Stop bragging!"

Some players, when they win, cannot control themselves. They jump for joy, screaming "I won! I won!" Or they dance about, chanting "You lose! You lose!" This does not portend well for future game playing. Intercede immediately by saying to the winner, "No one says you can't be happy you won, but try not to make everyone else feel bad that they didn't." Then turn to the offended player(s) and simply say, "He's proud of himself. You would be too. He shouldn't behave this way, though, and if you win next time, I'm sure you'll know how to act."

In this way you might actually manage to squelch a "payback." But don't bank on it. You're more likely to see an improvement once each player has crowed.

◆

◆ Snowball Bull's-Eye ◆

(AGES 4 AND UP)

2 or more players

Materials:
cardboard bull's-eye target
snowballs

Object of the Game:
To score the most points by hitting high-scoring sections of a target.

How to Play:

Sometimes snowball throwing can get too wild and players end up going home in tears. Taking aim at a target with snowballs definitely beats taking aim at other people. No one gets hurt, but everyone gets to throw his or her hardest and fastest. Target throwing is a great alternative to coming face-to-face with a hard-packed snowball.

Make a target on a piece of cardboard cut from the side of a box. Draw a red center for the 50-point bull's-eye. Around the center, draw four different-colored rings. The outside ring is worth 10 points, next is 20 points, next is 30 points, and next is 40 points. Tack the target on a tree or a fence post, or lean it against a wall where there are no windows. Mark a throwing line about ten to twenty feet back from the target. Each player makes three snowballs for each turn. Keep score by points or just keep count of how many bull's-eyes are hit. The player who scores the most points or who is the first to score five bull's-eyes is the winner.

Different Ages, Different Stages:

Keep in the mind the different ages of players when the throwing line is being determined. Younger players will naturally need to move closer to the target. To find the right distance for the line, have each player throw a practice snowball just to make sure he or she is capable of reaching the target. Try counting the rings marked 40 and 50 as a bull's-eye for younger players.

Then Try This!

Target-making time can also be a craft time. Get creative with what might be fun to aim for—a monster's face, a clown's nose, or even a picture of various things that are good to say no to—cigarettes, fatty foods, too much television. Make the target shape first, then add the artwork and the target circles on top of the art.

◆ No-Sled Snow-Sled Race ◆

2 or more players

Materials:
plastic garbage bag for each player
large cardboard box top or side for each player

Object of the Game:
To be the one who goes the farthest distance in a no-sled snow-sled race.

How to Play:
When racing down a snowy hill on a saucer or sled has gotten to be all too predictable, let players try sledding without the sled!

Give each player a plastic garbage bag and a side or top of a cardboard box (or any other flat, smooth thing that will easily come between the player's bottom and the snow). Each player starts at the same point at the top of the hill. Players sit down on the bag or box and wait for the start. At the word "Go!" they push off and put their feet up onto the bag or box. The player who goes the farthest wins the race. Best three out of five runs wins the tournament.

Different Ages, Different Stages:
As with all races, finish lines and starting lines may be adjusted to be closer for younger racers. Older players may not move as swiftly because of their weight. Before an official race begins, players should do a trial run just to see what distance adjustments should be made for the sake of fairness.

Then Try This!
All kinds of objects may be tried for sleds. Plastic lunch trays, garbage can lids without handles on top, or homemade plywood sleds that have been sanded and polyurethaned are some

other possible sled ideas. Kids can be "sled consumer guides," conducting tests on each kind of no-sled sled. Make test forms that include categories for comfort, speed, smoothness of ride, looks, and durability. Grade each category with a score from 1 to 5, with 5 being the highest grade.

FRE-E-E-E-E-ZING FUN!

Ice guys finish first with this trio of easy, freezey fun ideas. If the freezing cold is keeping players bored stiff and inside, let them in on the activities in this section. They're just the right mixture of chilly silliness for those icky, icy days.

◆ Painless Windowpane Painting ◆

(AGES 3 AND UP)

1 or more players

Materials:
frosty windows

Object of the Project:
To draw pictures and secret messages in the frost or condensation on the windowpanes on a cold day.

How to Play:
There's nothing to it. Just do it! When the cold is keeping people in, make use of some of the side effects of the frosty weather by suggesting windowpane painting and secret message writing.

Siblings can play alone or together. All that's needed is a "paintbrush" finger to scrape away the frost or condensation. Make a game of it by having one person draw a secret symbol or message on one window in the house. The other player must then find the message window, and in the course of the hunt leave another message to be found by the other player.

Different Ages, Different Stages:
Younger players will just enjoy making drawings. Older players can make up games to play with younger ones. The secret message game can be changed to "Find the Smile Face" or anything else. The older sibling can draw the face on any window. The younger one must then search the windows in the house to find the smile.

Then Try This!
When the secret messages have all been found, players can change the activity to drawing designs, writing their names, or playing tic-tac-toe in the frost.

Argument Ender #13

"We always play what *you* want to play!"

Usually, one sibling is more aggressive and less flexible about what he or she will play than another. And occasionally the more acquiescent of the two will rebel. When this happens suggest that they switch to another game for a brief while, and then, if they're both in the mood, return to the one that is now being insisted upon. If this does not appease the more demanding player, try asking, "If your brother doesn't want to play, he's not going to be fun to play with. So what's the point of forcing him?" There really is no good answer to this question. Either they will select another game or they'll be forced to play on their own.

◆

◆ Snowballs Forever ◆

1 or more players

Materials:
plastic bags
freezer
snow

Object of the Project:
To make and save snowballs for the future.

How to Play:
Players who like to plan ahead and have fun now too will like this cool idea. On a snowy day, take time out from snowman making to sculpt some perfect snowballs in all different sizes. Put them in plastic bags and hide them away in the freezer. Then forget about them until spring or summer. Imagine the surprise on a bright sunny day when snowballs are brought out for play!

Different Ages, Different Stages:
Everyone can make snowballs to freeze and keep. When the time comes to take the snowballs out, they will be more like ice balls. They should not be used by children of any age for snowball fights. However, they may be used for Snowball Bull's-eye or for water play in the kiddie pool.

Then Try This!
Before freezing snowballs, color them! Add a few drops of food coloring to a paper cup full of water. Drizzle the colored water over the snow and make a colored snowball.

◆ Chapter 7 ◆

Sick of Being Sick

Boredom Blasters

ILLNESSES ARE ENOUGH to make one sick! Sick of being sick, that is. It's bad enough to feel bad, but it's even worse to feel bad, bored, and stuck in bed. Siblings who share a room are sometimes forced to move out when germs move in. And sometimes the move isn't made fast enough and whatever one sibling has, the other one gets too. And although boredom is often the side effect of any illness, a little understanding on the part of both the sick and the well helps a lot. Activities made to be played in bed, on a bed, or from the safe distance of the doorway help even more. Here's just what the doctor ordered to cure those boredom blues.

GET BUSY, GET BETTER

Don't just lie there. Do something! Here is a collection of ideas that will keep even the most unhappy patient pleasantly preoccupied. From highly personalized get-well cards to sending sympathetic messages through the air, here are some chances for a sick kid to cheer up in a big way!

◆ Get-Well-Quick Card Craft ◆

(AGES 5 AND UP)

1 or more players

Materials:
construction paper
colored markers and crayons
white glue
scissors
decorative craft items (buttons, sequins, feathers, etc.).

Object of the Project:
To make homemade get-well cards.

How to Play:
A sick get-well wisher's greatest wish is to get well quickly. Why wait for the mail to bring get-well wishes from the outside world? Let the shut-in pass the time by filling his or her own sickroom with homemade get-well cards.

Spread the materials out on a lap tray if the player is stuck in bed, or on a table if he or she feels well enough to be up and around. First make the card by folding construction paper in half and then in half again. Use markers or crayons to draw a design on the cover and inside. Write funny or serious messages such as "I Hope I Get Well Soon!" Glue on decorative craft items to dress up the card. Make a bunch of them and set them up on the dresser, the night table, and the desk. Making cards fills the time and the room with cheeriness when it is needed most.

Different Ages, Different Stages:

Whether one person in the family is sick or all are sick, craft activities take minds off the discomfort and focus thoughts on creating something instead. Safety scissors, tape instead of glue, crayons instead of markers, and assistance from an older sibling make any craft activity safer and more fun for a young child. Older children can make fancier cards by cutting the cards into shapes and adding more three-dimensional decorations to them.

Then Try This!

While cards are being made, take the opportunity to make a box full of cards for all occasions. Suggest that the children make birthday cards to go on friends' birthday presents, or thank-you cards to be sent to grandparents or anyone else who deserves thanks at a later date. Cards for all occasions will come in handy and will even save money. Older children might be paid a small amount per card if they make cards for the card box.

◆ Creative TV Watching ◆

(AGES 8 AND UP)

1 or more players

Materials:

pencil and paper
television

Object of the Game:

To watch television with the purpose of developing observation skills.

How to Play:

If watching television is the only thing a sick player feels like doing, add an extra element of value to the activity. Even at a time when "there's nothing good on TV," some good can be made of the time spent watching. Keep a pencil and paper handy and be on the lookout for the following things:

1. How many commercials are on during a half-hour-long program? _____
2. How many cartoon shows feature animals as main characters? _____
3. How many child actors have red hair? _____
4. How many commercials make men look stupid?
   _____
5. How many commercials make women look stupid?
   _____
6. How many commercials make animals do impossible things such as talk and dance? _____
7. How many shows feature families with a mother and father raising children together in the same house?
   _____
8. How many shows feature a single father raising children alone? _____
9. How many shows feature a single mother raising children alone? _____
10. How many situation comedy shows feature a cast with one easygoing person, one stupid person, one gruff and mean person, and one totally wacko person?

    _____

Make up other questions to fit the player's television watching tastes.

Different Ages, Different Stages:

Older and younger players can develop their viewer awareness skills together. While watching a show, have the younger players look for simpler, more concrete details such as: How many boys and how many girls? How many children are wearing red? Blue? Green? How many children aren't really singing along when the main character is leading the group in a song?

Then Try This!

When a child is sick and discovers that daytime television has little to offer, turn off the sound and watch in silence. The viewer can see how much he or she is able to tell about what's going on with only the actions as a guide. Turn the sound up again after five minutes and see how much of the story was understood without the words.

◆ Cheer-Up Pillowcase ◆

(AGES 4 AND UP)

1 or more players

Materials:
plain pillowcase
shirt cardboard
fabric markers

Object of the Project:
To make a pillowcase to be used on sick days.

How to Play:
When sickness makes bed the only place to be, this craft activity adds some cheerful fun to an otherwise boring sickbed.

Let the patient create his or her own special cheer-up pillowcase. A plain pillowcase spread out on a lap tray can be dressed up and decorated with colorful fabric markers. Before using the markers, slip a shirt cardboard inside the case to absorb excess marker ink. Some ideas for cheerful designs are: a big yellow smile face, or lots of little ones all over the case; balloons of all colors floating on the case; hearts; flowers; butterflies; rainbows; kittens; kites; or any other designs that would cheer up the patient.

Different Ages, Different Stages:
Older siblings can be helpful to younger ones by drawing outlines of designs for the younger ones to color in. Younger and

114

older siblings can work together on such ideas as having the younger one lay his or her hand flat out on the pillowcase while the older one draws an outline of the hand. Little hand outlines all over the case may then be colored in for a very cheerful design.

Then Try This!
An autograph pillowcase makes a very special present to a child who has been out of class for a while due to illness. Write a get-well message in the center of the pillowcase. Then have each class member sign his or her name in colored marker. Deliver the case along with a handmade get-well card and the effects are sure to be cheerful!

◆ Plane and Simple Messages ◆
(AGES 3 AND UP)

2 or more players

Materials:
paper (8½" × 11")
paper clips
pencils or pens

Object of the Game:
To make paper airplanes and send messages back and forth without getting too close to the sick person.

How to Play:
When sickness makes close contact a forbidden thing, siblings can still wish each other well by sending messages back and forth from doorway to bedside on paper airplanes. Here are some easy instructions for making a simple paper plane.

Follow the steps and refer to the illustrations for making the perfect message plane.

1. Write a message on an 8½" × 11" piece of paper.
2. Fold the paper in half the long way.

115

3. Open up the paper and fold each half three times, as shown in the illustrations. Make the folds meet the crease in the middle of the paper.
4. Open up the wings and hold the center triangular fold between two fingers.
5. Place a paper clip under the nose of the plane, toward the tip of it. This will weight the plane so it will fly.
6. Send the message soaring!

Different Ages, Different Stages:
Older siblings can make the planes for the younger ones. But all ages can do the message writing, picture coloring, or just plane decorating of the plain pieces of paper. All ages will enjoy zooming the planes back and forth.

Then Try This!
Set up one wastepaper basket by the bed of the sick sibling and another one at the doorway where the well sibling stands at a safe distance from germs. Each player tries to fly paper planes into the basket at the opposite end of the "runway."

◆ Sick Joke to Play ◆
(AGES 8 AND UP)

1 or more players

Materials:
red nontoxic marker (the kind that washes off)
mirror

Object of the Project:
To amuse one who is sick and those who are taking care of him or her.

How to Play:
Practical jokes may not always be practical, but they are often pretty funny. Someone who is sick may not be too sick to play

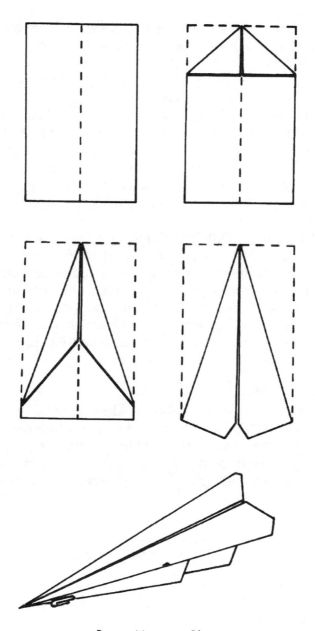

Paper Message Plane

a sick joke on a brother or sister who comes into the sickroom to visit. Here is one joke that's sure to add a laugh and a half to the sickroom.

Just before it's time for a helpful sibling to bring in a glass of fresh juice or a bowl of chicken soup, the patient should pick up a mirror and a red marker. While looking in the mirror, he or she may add red dots all over the face and body. When the caretaker arrives to check on the patient, surprise! A rash to end all rashes! After the initial response, which is sure to be amazement, the patient can reveal the joke and invite the sibling to join in a game of connect the dots!

Different Ages, Different Stages:
Jokes like this one are made to be played on an older audience. Very young children won't get the joke, and those a little bit older may resent being fooled. However, older children can include younger siblings in the fun by allowing them to help do the dotting with a promise to keep a straight face while they both play the sick joke on a parent or other sibling. It's all in fun, of course.

Then Try This!
While in the mood for sick jokes, children home sick may find it is fun to make silly signs for the front door or sickroom door. Signs like ENTER AT YOUR OWN RISK! or ALL GIFTS WELCOME! will get a laugh every time and will give the patient something to do when there's nothing to do except sniffle, sneeze, scratch, and wheeze.

PENCIL SHARPENERS

Being sick can be a real pain. Dull that pain with a sharp pencil and a few good pencil games to play right in the comfort of the couch or bed. These classic pencil wit sharpeners provide quiet fun for siblings who are stuck at home with a sniffle, a sneeze, or some other boredom-producing disease. They won't get siblings worked up, but they will get them working together.

◆ Pyramid Power ◆

2 or 3 players

Materials:

pencil and paper (a different color pencil for each player works
well in this game)

Object of the Game:

To complete and initial as many triangles on the game board
as possible. The player who completes a triangle is the one who
initials it.

How to Play:

To set up, draw a game board on a blank sheet of paper, making
six rows of dots, as shown (see illustration). The first player
draws a line connecting two adjacent dots diagonally or hori-

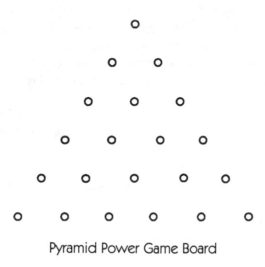

Pyramid Power Game Board

119

zontally. The second player connects two more dots, and so it continues with each turn. However, when a player completes a triangle he or she claims it by putting an initial inside it. The game continues until all the dots are connected and all possible triangles are made. The player with the most initialed triangles wins.

◆ Boxes ◆

(4 AND UP)

2 or 3 players

Materials:
pencil and paper (a different color pencil for each player works well in this game)

Object of the Game:
To complete and initial as many boxes as possible.

How to Play:
This is a variation of Pyramid Power. Instead of drawing a game board in the shape of a pyramid, draw this game board in the shape of a rectangle. On a blank sheet of paper, draw six rows of six dots about one inch apart, as shown (see illustration). The first player draws a line connecting two adjacent dots horizontally or vertically. The second player connects two more dots, and so it continues with each turn. As a player completes a box, he or she claims it by putting an initial inside it. The game continues until all the dots are connected and all possible boxes are made. The player with the most initialed boxes wins.

Different Ages, Different Stages:
Start out by creating a game board made of three rows of dots. Space the lines far apart. Let the younger sibling practice with this simplified version until he or she is comfortable with the bigger board.

Boxes Game Board

Then Try This!

Finished game boards for both Pyramid Power and Boxes make fun coloring projects. Give younger siblings crayons, colored pencils, or markers for coloring in the boxes and triangles. It's good practice for small motor skills, and the results are colorful designs that will impress young artists with their own ability.

◆ Alphabet Art ◆

(AGES 4 AND UP)

1 or more players

Materials:
pencil and paper

Object of the Game:
To create a recognizable drawing using any letter of the alphabet as the basis for the drawing.

How to Play:
Use this game to teach the alphabet to young children and encourage artistic creativity in children of all ages at the same

time. Start with the letter *A* or choose any letter of the alphabet. Draw or write the letter anywhere on the paper. Draw around the letter, using it as a part of your drawing. A simple example would be the letter *O*, which could easily be turned into a face by adding eyes, nose, and mouth. If only one player is playing, then the object is to meet the challenge of turning a letter into some other thing. If two players are playing, when the drawings are completed, each player can take turns guessing the identity of the other's drawing. The player who identifies the other's drawing in the fewest number of guesses wins.

Different Ages, Different Stages:
Have each player select a letter for the other player. Letters with complex shapes are more difficult to incorporate into a drawing.

Then Try This!
Make a collage of all the letters.

Argument Ender #14

"Timmy and my brother won't play with me!"

All siblings have the right to play alone with a friend sometimes. Unfortunately, it often happens that siblings are playing fast and furiously and then suddenly a friend pops by. Seconds later one sibling is left almost literally picking up the pieces while the other goes off to have a high old time. If the child whose friend has dropped by is in the middle of a game with a sibling, gently insist that he or she finish it while the friend watches, assuring that once it's done he or she can go off. Then either find the other child someone else to play with or get him or her settled with a solitary activity. Do not insist that they all play together. It isn't fair and it won't work.

◆

◆ Creature Features ◆

3 or more players

Materials:
crayons or markers
paper

Object of the Game:
To work together to create a silly creature with extraordinary features.

How to Play:
Players don't have to be great artists to have a great time in this drawing game. As soon as your children are old enough to hold a crayon and not eat it, they will have fun creating joint pictures that are sure to get the giggles going.

This is one game in which artistic ability has little to do with the amount of satisfaction gained from playing. Older siblings may be better at filling in details on a drawing, but even the scribbles of the youngest player can add a silly touch to the drawings. Get ready for the game by folding a piece of paper into thirds. As each player takes a turn, he or she should be careful not to let the other player see the drawing. Starting at the top third of the piece of paper, the first player or artist begins by drawing the head of an imaginary creature. This head may be silly, scary, or realistic. When the player is done, he or she should fold the paper back so only a tiny part of the drawing shows. The next player then draws the middle section of the creature, adding the body and part of the arms. When this player is finished, the middle third of the paper should be folded back so no part of the drawing shows. The final third of the paper is then filled in by the third player, who finishes the creature by adding legs and feet. When the drawing is complete, the last artist unfolds it to reveal the finished masterpiece creature feature (see illustration on the next page).

123

Creature Feature

Different Ages, Different Stages:

When the drawings are completed, younger siblings will enjoy being the official "color-inners." Hand out the crayons to the young ones and let them put the finishing touches on all the creations.

Then Try This!

Try the same game using words to describe characters instead of a drawing. Fold the paper in thirds. The first player writes a description of the character's face. The second player adds a description of the middle part of the character. The third player finishes off the description. Read aloud the final description and listen to the laughs!

♦ Chapter 8 ♦

The Gang's All Here

Fun for Sets of Siblings

GROUPS WON'T GRIPE if they have something fun to do together. In a house where children of different ages live, friends of different ages are sure to show up at the same time sometimes. Also, when your adult friends visit with their children, things can get very wild! When a gang of mixed ages arrives for a planned party or a casual visit, these group activities will make everyone a part of the good-times family-and-friends gang.

ALL FOR FUN

There's no such thing as too many, too young, or too old when it comes to playing the games in this section. Bring on the visiting cousins, the sibling's friends, and the new kids across the street. The more the merrier because they're all in it together.

◆ Talent Show Time ◆

4 or more players

Materials:
props to be determined by each act
audience (can be imaginary)

Object of the Project:
To showcase talent and entertain an audience.

How to Play:
Everyone has a talent of some kind. It's just a matter of finding what each player does best. A talent show is a variety show that allows everyone to show off his or her very best abilities. For one it may be playing a musical instrument, for another dancing a ballet routine, and for another displaying great basketball skills. Telling jokes, singing a song, and demonstrating how the Hula Hoop works are all "talents" that make a show a real audience pleaser.

Here are some other ideas for acts:

• *Imitate the Famous*—Sing like Barney, talk like Donald Duck, walk like Charlie Chaplin, or dress up like a famous actor or actress and imitate his or her most famous lines and motions.

• *Lip-Synch Sing-Along*—Play a recording of a favorite song. Dress up in a wild outfit and sing along without really singing.

• *The Great Houdunit*—Perform real easy-to-do magic tricks found in magic books, or play the role of the wacky magician who never seems to get a trick to work right.

• *Can You Kazoo Band*—Anyone who can hum a tune can play a kazoo. Form a kazoo band and kazoo a few tunes for the audience.

• *Performing Pets*—Let the animals get into the act. Just ask a dog or cat to do whatever it has been trained to do. Add music to the performance and listen to the audience howl with appreciation.

127

Different Ages, Different Stages:
When it comes to putting on a show of any kind, the more players the better. Older players can create curtains from old sheets hung over a clothesline, cue cards announcing each act, and programs to hand out to the audience. Younger players can help by holding the cue cards, drawing back the curtain, and handing out programs. Everyone can be a part of the performing cast. Little players may sing, dance, do tumbling, or just make silly faces. Older players may take the opportunity to show off what they've learned in lessons or sports programs. In a talent show, anything goes.

Then Try This!
Turn the talent show into a moneymaking event. Create advertising posters and put them up around the neighborhood. Sell tickets in advance. At the show, sell popcorn and drinks. Make this an annual neighborhood event.

◆ Easy Indoor Olympics ◆
(AGES 8 AND UP)

4 or more players

Materials:
medals made of construction paper
scorecards with numbers 1 through 10 for each judge
additional materials to be determined by specific events

Object of the Game:
To compete in various relay races to win "Olympic" medals.

How to Play:
Invite all the kids in the neighborhood to participate in this event. Select two or more participants to be judges and give each judge a set of scorecards numbered from 1 through 10. Choose a wide-open space for the games. Divide the players into two teams, or compete individually. As the games are

played, the judges will hold up their scorecards and the scores will be added up to find the final score. Races and relay races make good events. Here are just some ideas for Olympic-type games to play:

• *The Crawl*—Players line up behind a starting line. They lie on the ground, prop themselves up on their hands, and then "walk" on their hands to the finish line, dragging legs and feet behind them. First to finish wins 10 points. Judges give extra points for style.

• *The Sack*—Players line up behind the starting line. Each player stands inside a burlap bag or a plastic garbage bag, holding it up around his or her waist. Players must hop to the finish line. First to finish wins 10 points. Judges give extra points for style.

• *Between the Knees*—Materials needed to play this are two beach balls, two books, and two teams, equal in number. The two teams line up behind the starting line, standing in two parallel lines, with one player from each team going first. The first player in each line begins with a beach ball held between the knees and a book balanced on top of the head. At the start signal, both carefully race to the finish line, trying not to drop either the ball or the book. If anything is dropped, the player must start over. At the finish line, the player carries the book and ball back to the next teammate on the starting line. The first team to finish the whole line wins 10 points. Judges give extra points for style.

• *The Jump*—Players take a running start and at a designated line they jump as far as possible. The player who jumps the longest distance wins 10 points. Judges give extra points for style.

Different Ages, Different Stages:

Children under the age of 8 may not be able to do some of the suggested games—however, there's no reason not to set up some games appropriate for the younger players in the group. A simple running race, crawling race, or hopping-on-two-feet race will get the young ones involved. Let them help by handing out cups of water to the older players as well as by being the official cheering squad.

Then Try This!
Play music, have an "Olympics parade" with players carrying flags made of T-shirts tied to sticks, and have an awards ceremony at the end of the events. A big family picnic would top off the day very nicely!

Argument Ender #15

"They won't let me play! They say I'm too little!"

Sometimes when there is one child who is significantly younger than the rest he or she is treated at best like a nonentity and at worst like a pariah. The games in this chapter, however, are suitable in some way for every age. Simply take the youngest child by the hand, go over to the group, and firmly say, "Let's all think of something Thomas can do." Then offer a few suggestions that make it clear you want to protect the older kids' fun, but do expect that they will engage him in some nonintrusive way. Once a solution is found, hang around for a minute or two. Make sure that Thomas is indeed doing his bit without unknowingly botching things up for the other players, and that the rest of the kids are allowing him his role. Then go back and enjoy your own friends.

◆ Stop and Swap ◆
(AGES 4 AND UP)

2 or more players

Materials:
trading items, (old toys, books, stickers, baseball cards, cassette tapes, CDs, posters, comic books, etc.)

Object of the Game:

To have a group swap day. Players trade and recycle used items on a temporary or permanent basis.

How to Play:

The idea of trading instead of discarding is a good lesson in recycling and stretching the lifetime of outgrown items. Trading used items for other used items is a great way to get something "new" without having to spend any money. With a little advance notice, a group of players can get together and have the fun of "shopping" by swapping items with each other. Visiting children can bring along a bag full of items they'd like to throw onto the trading table. Siblings can select items from their own belongings.

When the group is all together, items for swapping should be displayed on a swap-shop table. Since no money changes hands and it is impossible to put a monetary value on used items, it should be made clear that all items are considered to be of equal trade value. Trades can be made on a permanent or a temporary basis. If trades are to be temporary, the items should be labeled with the owners' names, addresses, the date of the trades, and the dates when traded items are to be returned. Set a length-of-loan time—two weeks, for example—and make a lending card for each item. An index card file can be kept for each item to keep track of who has traded with whom. If trades are permanent, there should also be a trade-back rule that allows three days for minds to change.

Different Ages, Different Stages:

Younger siblings and friends may not be ready for permanent exchanges. Let the little ones play "shopping" with the knowledge that all items will be returned at the end of the playtime.

Older siblings and friends can take the swapping more seriously by making up lending cards to be filled out with each swap. A card might look like the sample on the next page.

```
Cassette tape: _____
Swapper: _____
Shopper: _____
Date swapped: _____
Date due back: _____
```

Then Try This!

Have a group tag sale. Let all the swappers and shoppers gather together items they would like to sell. Set up a table outside where pedestrian traffic can see that there's a sale going on. Put up Tag Sale posters around the neighborhood telling the time, date, and place of the sale. Let the players be responsible for their own sale items, or just divide the money up evenly when the sale is over.

◆ Balloon Bop Contest ◆

(AGES 4 AND UP)

3 or more players

Materials:

balloons
string

Object of the Game:

To pop other players' balloons while avoiding having one's own balloon popped.

How to Play:

This game is one that's sure to be *pop-ular* with a whole gang of siblings and friends who don't mind the sound of balloons popping. Everyone can play.

Blow up enough balloons so that each person playing has one. Attach a long string to each balloon and tie one balloon around one ankle of each player. At the word "Go!" players try to pop the other players' balloons without breaking his or her own. No hands are allowed, so the only way to pop balloons is to stomp on them. The last player to have his or her own balloon popped is the winner.

Argument Ender #16

"Everyone is ganging up on me!"

A bunch of kids will sometimes gang up on one child. Sometimes it's deserved, other times it's just a classic moment of childhood "cruelty." In any event it's no way to work out a problem or express a darker side, and should obviously not be allowed. Step into the fray and ask someone what the problem seems to be. Then encourage the person who is being attacked to state his or her case. If there is wrongdoing on both sides, encourage apologies, suggest that everyone literally shake out the bad energy (see "Shake on It" in chapter 9), and suggest that once they do this they go back to playing. If one person has been wrongfully attacked, don't make the other side grovel. Something short and sweet will do. Suggest they all say they are sorry. Then, since awkwardness is bound to follow, take over for a minute or two with a lot of talk. Ask questions about what's being swapped, line kids up for the "olympics," or start giving out costumes. Get everyone's mind off the altercation as quickly as you can. Each child will be grateful and in short order you'll be able to sidle away.

◆

Different Ages, Different Stages:
Younger players will pay more attention to popping other play-ers' balloons than to guarding their own. If older players seem to have the popping advantage, allow the younger ones two balloons before they are out of the game.

Then Try This!
Turn the Balloon Bop into a Balloon Bop Hop. Turn on some music that makes players feel like dancing. As they dance they also try to pop other players' balloons.

◆ Suitcase Relay ◆

(AGES 4 AND UP)

4 or more players

Materials:
2 suitcases filled with equal amounts of clothing items (long dresses, big suit jackets, hats, gloves, big boots, pants, etc.)

Object of the Game:
For one team to be the first to complete the relay race of trying on funny clothes and taking them off again.

How to Play:
Fill two suitcases with an equal amount of clothing items. Be-cause these clothes will be put on over players' regular clothes, it is a good idea to use large-size clothing. Divide the group into two equal teams. If there is an uneven number, then one player on the team with fewer players must take two turns. The two teams form two lines at the opposite end of the room from where the suitcases are. On the word "Go!" the first person in each line must run to a suitcase, open it, and put on all the clothes in it over the clothes he or she is already wearing. Then the player must take off the suitcase clothes, put them back in the suitcase, close it up, and run back to the line. The next

players do the same until everyone has had a turn. The first team to finish is the winning team.

Different Ages, Different Stages:
A different set of suitcases might be set out for the younger players, who have more trouble putting on clothes. Fill the suitcases with items that are easier to get in and out of (hats, mittens, sunglasses, jackets, or scarves, for example). The older the players, the more items may be packed in the suitcases.

Then Try This!
Play the same game, but require that all items be put on backward! It's a little more difficult and it looks a lot funnier.

◆ Last Laps ◆
(ALL AGES)

The more players, the merrier

Materials:
sturdy chair

Object of the Game:
To stack as many seated players as possible on a chair.

How to Play:
Players will all be the last to laugh no matter whose lap is last. Choose a sturdy chair and place it in an open area with space around it. The first person sits in the chair and the second person sits in the lap of the first person. Add a third, fourth, fifth, and however many more can manage to climb up on the last lap without toppling over the lap stack.

Different Ages, Different Stages:
This is one game in which size matters more than age, so the biggest player should be the first seated. The lap pile should

get higher as the players get smaller and smaller. Very little ones should be the last on the laps and should be held securely.

Then Try This!

Last Laps is not unlike one fad of the 1960s, when college students tried to see how many of them could squeeze into a phone booth. Other such contests that would be appropriate for children would be to see how many can fit in an inflated kiddie pool minus the water, or how many players can stand in a circle with their backs facing each other and their elbows linked. Once linked in the circle the players move all at once in any direction. It's not easy, but a good laugh is sure to be had by all.

◆ Chapter 9 ◆

Fence Menders

Games to Play and Things to Say for the "Not Speaking"

WHEN FITS AND FIGHTS turn a happy home into a sibling war zone, bring peace and relief with some games and activities designed to mend friendship fences and break down the walls of silence between two "not speaking" siblings. The object of these peace-restoring ideas is to provide a safe way to let out some aggression, a successful way to ward off false accusations during play, and a chance to laugh away the anger within.

FENCE MENDERS

Children who are fighting lose the benefit of having a playmate. Anger and tears may replace camaraderie and laughter. The whole mood of the home may be dark and gloomy because the siblings within are positively furious at each other. Bring the joy back by helping the squabblers work out their troubles together in games that allow them to express their feelings and relieve the tension physically. These are helpful icebreakers that acknowledge the problems and begin solving them.

◆ Paper Bag Popping ◆

2 or more players

Materials:
paper lunch bags

Object of the Game:
To make a loud popping noise by smashing paper bags with a hand.

How to Play:
When anger stops the fun, stop the anger with a game that brings fast relief. Give each player an equal number of paper lunch bags. Standing six to ten feet apart, players fill a bag with air by holding the top loosely closed and blowing into the bag. When the bag is full, players hold it tightly closed and pop it with the free hand. Fill another bag with air and pop it. Continue popping bags until the anger is forgotten and replaced with laughter.

Different Ages, Different Stages:
Siblings who relieve their anger by hitting each other will feel the same relief by popping the bags in the same room, glaring directly at each other! Younger siblings may need a parent to blow up the bags for them.

Then Try This!
Broken paper bags may be balled up and used as ammunition in the Ready, Aim, Fire! game, later in this chapter.

◆ A Penny for Your Thoughts ◆

2 or more players

Materials:
penny

Object of the Game:
To give each person an opportunity to tell his or her side of the story without interruption.

How to Play:
Sometimes all it takes to end a dispute is a fair chance to be heard. This game comes in very handy when siblings are shouting at each other and no one is really listening. When a shouting match begins, end it this way. Toss a penny in the air and have each player call heads or tails. The winner holds the penny and begins to tell his or her side of the story about what started the argument. The other player may not interrupt. When the first player has finished, the penny is handed over to the other player. Then that player tells his or her version of what happened without being interrupted. The penny is passed back and forth between the players until both have had their say. Players may not repeat themselves on their turns. They must say each thing only once. Eventually, both will run out of something to say. Then the penny is tossed again, with the players again calling heads or tails. The winner of the toss must then say one nice thing about the other player. The coin is passed back and forth until each player has said three nice things about the other.

Different Ages, Different Stages:
Instead of being allowed to ramble on endlessly, younger players should be encouraged to hold the penny and state one fact about what started the argument. Then the penny should be turned over to the other player.

Then Try This!

Even a small argument and one not worth arguing, can interfere with playtime fun. Solve the problems quickly with one penny. Toss the coin for heads or tails. The player who wins the toss wins the right to be right.

◆ Ready, Aim, Fire! ◆

(AGES 4 AND UP)

2 or more players

Materials:

scrap paper (sheets of newspaper, used typing paper, old wrapping paper, etc.)
2 wastebaskets

Object of the Game:

To release anger with the physical motion of throwing paper into a basket.

How to Play:

Being cooped up in the house too long can bring on a need for releasing physical energy. If siblings start expressing this need by hitting one another, bring out the box of "stress paper" and the empty wastebaskets. Give each sibling an equal pile of paper and a wastebasket. Place the baskets no more than five feet from each player. Then encourage the players to put their energy into balling up pieces of paper and throwing them into their target baskets. Allow them to express their anger verbally as each throw is made, but the words must be directed to the baskets instead of one another. "Ready, aim, fire!" they might say as they ball up the paper and prepare to throw. Or "Take that!" "You make me so mad!" "I'll get you for that!" The anger will subside gradually as the players use up their negative energy.

Different Ages, Different Stages:
The game itself should not be made frustrating by having the target baskets too far away. Each player should be able to easily sink the "balls" in the basket.

Then Try This!
Take turns trying to hit the other person's paper ball in midair before it reaches the basket.

◆ Squirt Gun Fun ◆

2 players

Materials:
squirt gun for each player
water

Object of the Game:
To hit each other with water instead of hands or words.

How to Play:
When siblings seem to be as steaming mad as two wet hens, let them really cool off and wash away their anger. Give each player a loaded squirt gun and have them stand back to back with squirt guns down at their sides. The squirt gun duel begins at the word "Go!" from a third party. Players each take ten long, slow steps in opposite directions. At the end of the ten steps, they both wait for the command from the caller to "Turn and fire!" Both players turn and squirt water at each other. The winner of the duel is the one who hits the other with water. Continue the squirt gun fun with a squirt gun fight that has both players running to avoid the other's stream.

Different Ages, Different Stages:
In a duel with a significantly younger player, each person should take only five long steps away from the other. Before

saying "Turn and fire!" the caller should add "One, two, three" in order to give the younger player time to prepare.

Then Try This!

If tempers are too hot to withstand such a civilized solution as a duel, divide the play area into two territories with a clearly defined border. Players must try to invade the other's territory, either by foot or with a stream of water from a squirt gun. Players guard their borders by squirting each other. A player who gets wet while trying to cross a border must allow the other player a free squirt.

◆ Corner Warmers ◆

(AGES 3 AND UP)

2 or more players

Materials:

separate corner per player
timer or stopwatch

Object of the Game:

To settle an argument without the help of a parent.

How to Play:

Even in professional fights the players get sent back to their separate corners between rounds. When siblings need to take a break from their fight, put each of them in a separate corner, backs facing out. Set a timer for three minutes and tell the siblings there will be no talking during that time. Instead they must each think of how the argument or fight might be settled without a parent's help. When the timer signals the end of the quiet time, the siblings must still face the corner as they begin to talk about their ideas for how to end the fight. If they cannot settle the argument, set the timer for another three minutes and try again. Eventually, they will tire of corner warming and will welcome the chance to play again.

142

Different Ages, Different Stages:
Older players may need a longer time-out. Set the timer for five minutes with no talking allowed.

Then Try This!
Give each corner warmer a pad of paper and a pencil. Instead of making them give their solutions aloud, let them write out their ideas or draw pictures expressing their thoughts.

◆ Shake on It ◆

(ALL AGES)

1 or more players

Materials:
none needed

Object of the Game:
To physically shake off the anger and frustration.

How to Play:
Whether a child is angry with a parent or with another sibling, this activity literally shakes off the anger and bad feelings. Anyone can do it, even a parent!

Stand perfectly still. Start shaking one hand. Shake it for about fifteen seconds. Start shaking the other hand too. Lift one foot, shake it, and put it down. Lift the other foot, shake it, and put it down. Shake the shoulders up and down. Shake the head to the left and right. Shake as many body parts as possible all at once. When the giggles take over the shakers, players should shake hands with each other.

Different Ages, Different Stages:
Older players, who might be too self-conscious to shake off anger in front of one another, should be encouraged to go into separate rooms and do this exercise alone. Shaking out limbs really is a good stress-buster that helps relax muscles and cools

down a hot temper. Add a couple of head rolls and finger stretches to get the kinks out of tensed-up areas.

Then Try This!
Turn on some fast music and start shaking along with the rhythm. Shaking will turn to dancing and the mood will turn from glum to glad.